MONEY GROW$
ON TREE$

MONEY GROW$ ON TREE$

HOW TO MAKE, MANAGE, AND MASTER MONEY

ALTON HOWARD

HOWARD
PUBLISHING CO.

3117 North 7th
West Monroe, Louisiana 71291

Illustrations by Kristen Myers
Cover Design by Steve Diggs & Friends

Howard Publishers
3117 North 7th Street, West Monroe, LA 71291-2227

Printed in the United States of America

First Printing, June 1991
Second Printing, August 1991

ISBN# 1-878990-16-0

To my lovely wife, Jean, who has been my number one supporter; to my two beautiful daughters, Mary and Janice, who have been my cheerleaders; to my son, John, who is also my partner in business and close advisor; to my sons-in-law, Mac and David and my daughter-in-law, Chrys, who are using their talents for the betterment of our world; to my grandchildren, Korie, Ryan, Ashley, Cherry, Callie, Jenna, and John David, who are my pride and joy. Also, to today's youth and the young at heart.

Contents

Section III: *Bringing It All Together*

Section IV: *Promoter's Paradise*

Summary: *A Final Look*

Appendix

About the Author

Alton H. Howard is . . . in both the vernacular and literal sense—"a country boy who done good." By the time he was twenty-one, he had gone from hunting possums to putting together profitable business deals.

Now, at age sixty-six, he's still going strong, unwilling to rest on the successes that have earned him millions. He's still dreaming, planning, and working on new projects that will stretch into the next century.

Born on a sixty-acre farm in the small community of Rocky Branch, Louisiana, Alton's youth was tremendously influenced by the deep Christian faith of his family and the tough times of the depression. Early in life, he learned the value of a dollar and the meaning of hard work.

Armed with his spiritual convictions and his dedicated work ethic, Alton rose from a stockroom clerk for F.W. Woolworth Co. in 1941 to the co-founder of the highly successful Howard Brothers Jewelers in 1946. Then in 1959 he co-founded Howard Brothers Discount Stores Inc., which ultimately grew to over 100 stores across the southern United States. The chain was sold in 1978.

In 1960 he co-founded Mid-South Development Company Inc., a shopping center and real estate development enterprise. And in 1970 Alton established Howard Publishing Company Inc., which publishes Christian books, hymnals, and music.

Alton re-entered the retail industry in 1984 by co-founding Super Saver Wholesale Warehouse Club Inc. Under his leadership as CEO, the chain rapidly expanded to twenty stores and reached astounding sales of a quarter of a billion dollars in three short years. These stores were sold in 1987 to Wal-Mart Stores, Inc. and became a part of Sam's Wholesale Clubs.

Alton Howard is a proven man, a rarity in the business world, and through this book, he provides proven methods for those who are fighting for freedom from financial struggles.

Acknowledgements

All I know, I have learned from someone else—who, where, and when, I cannot fully detail. Experiences, events, concepts; things I have heard, seen, and read; all have been a part of the process.

My first acknowledgement must be to my mother and father, who provided an umbrella of love and protection during my childhood and youth, and then to my dear wife, Jean, who has been my faithful companion for over forty-two years and who has made our home a happy haven. A special thanks goes to Philis Boultinghouse and my son John, who have been of invaluable help in editing and reviewing the contents of this book. To my friend, Sam Walton, for writing the foreword of this book. At a time in life when most would have checked out, he is still out encouraging his "troops," and, as he likes to say, "running his traps." Sam Walton's success story and his work ethics are an example and encouragement to us all. To the many other friends, associates, and even strangers, from whom I have learned, and to our benevolent heavenly Father, who gives life and sustenance to all, I give my thanks.

Foreword

by Sam Walton

For a number of years, I have known and admired Alton Howard, a servant-leader respected by the business community for his management talents and acts of humanitarianism. It is a privilege and honor to endorse this publication, which he has so capably authored.

In my opinion, there has never before been a greater need for instruction on how to be effective stewards of our resources. Alton Howard's visionary and quality characteristics, along with his sense of humor, have enabled him to develop a philosophy that is so essential to success: setting goals, being accountable, and above all—practicing honesty and integrity.

The fact that all men are created equal with the right to Life, Liberty and The Pursuit of Happiness does not assure us excellence in all walks of life. However, by applying the basic principles set forth in these chapters —a plan of action, discipline, compassion, and control— many worthwhile objectives can be achieved, whether from the standpoint of family budgeting or corporate financing.

The American Dream is still attainable. The doors of opportunity are wide open. Alton Howard's formula of moral values, coupled with the right attitude and a willingness to be a winner, can transform dreams into a wonderful life and a measure of accomplishment.

I highly recommend this book and believe you will enjoy and benefit from reading and studying this comprehensive text on managing money. We *can* make a difference and truly be whatever we choose to be.

Sam Walton
Chairman of the Board
Wal-Mart Stores, Inc.

Introduction

How do you measure wealth? Is wealth merely based on what you have earned, saved, and invested? What about the incalculable value of your health, your family, and your friends? Consider also the pleasure you receive in accomplishing your goals and successfully managing your life and the pride you feel in a job well done.

"Money Grows On Trees" is not only about putting dollars on your money tree, but also addresses the whole of life. The principles outlined in this book will teach you how to grow a bountiful money tree and much more.

Purpose
The purpose of this book is to help you:
1. Become debt free
2. Comprehend money management principles
3. Understand debt and its danger
4. See the importance of budgets and cash flow
5. Understand stewardship
6. Realize the value of establishing a savings plan
7. Understand investments
8. Learn basic stock market principles
9. Know how to avoid scams
10. Learn how to take advantage of opportunities
11. Realize the importance of a will

Empty Hands

Ninety-five percent of Americans reach retirement age with little or nothing to show for all their years of labor. The Bureau of Health and Human Resources reports that 85 percent of all Americans at age 65 have less than $250 in savings. Lack of preparation, ignorance, eroding morality, and a disregard for commitment are the main reasons for this dilemma. Of course, sometimes unfortunate circumstances and disaster are to blame. But why all the rest?

Who's to blame?

Ultimately, each individual must accept responsibility for their own financial condition. However, it must be conceded that there has been a shift in the overall direction of our country. The whole tenor of our government, schools, businesses, and citizenry once reflected foundational moral and ethical values.

Now, a new emphasis has infiltrated our whole society. Our current mentality says, "buy now, pay later," "you only go around once," and "do it your way." A large portion of our society have become consumers rather than producers. We are now reaping the whirlwind of the seed we have sown.

The Choice Is Yours

You do not have to be caught up in the mistakes around you. You have before you open doors of opportunity for success. You *can* grow a healthy, happy, and prosperous money tree. The choice is yours.

---

*Far too many are over the hill in earnings,
while just reaching their peak years of spending.*

SECTION I

Turning the Soil

CHAPTER ONE

Your Money Tree

He who gathers crops in summer
is a wise son,
but he who sleeps during harvest
is a disgraceful son.
— Proverbs 10:5

A little boy was asked, "What would you do if you were given all the money in the world?" He quickly responded, "I would pay off all my mama and daddy's debts—until the money ran out."

Debt is a killer, and most Americans are trapped in a no-win scenario. Actually, not all debt is wrong. It is the *purpose* for which the debt is incurred that is the determining factor.

Most everyone would like to be debt free, successful, happy, and financially secure. Psychologists tell us that peace of mind and prosperity are the ultimate goals of most people. Yet, few actually attain them.

Why is this so, and what can you do to beat the odds? There are certain principles and laws that govern success. Those who are ignorant of these rules (or simply ignore them) will always wonder why everything seems to go wrong for them.

3

This book is written out of fifty years of tough business and personal experience. During that time, God has blessed my efforts, and I have made several million; but I have also succeeded in losing several thousand along the way. Fortunately, the pluses have outweighed the minuses. I can attest to the value of heeding good money-management principles. I only wish I had known them a bit sooner in my own life. All our tombstones could probably read: "Too soon old, too late smart."

Whether you are a homemaker, factory worker, business executive, plumber, or street sweeper, these principles of money management apply to you, and they will bring you success if you apply them consistently. But remember, success is a relative term. It is measured not only in terms of dollars in the bank, but also by the quality of one's "spiritual bank account." Your relationships with others, your purpose in life, and your level of commitment and contentment are strong indicators of true success.

The truth of the matter, however, is that all these elements are enormously affected by one's financial management skills. The lack of sound financial responsibility can ruin your life.

The burden of debt, as a result of mismanagement, is one of the leading causes of family squabbles, break-ups, physical and mental illness, suicide, crime, wasted talent, and lost productivity. I have observed this to be true in my many years as a businessman, as a church elder, and through my personal involvement in counseling others.

Tell It Like It Is

Up front I want to tell you that the principles I will be discussing have a biblical base. I realize that some readers may be "turned-off" by religion. Some evangelists promise that Christianity is all "blue skies." They say that all you have to do is send in $100, then sit back and wait for the postman to deliver *you* $1,000. This philosophy is neither true nor biblical.

You may have had a bad religious experience, but that is no reason to disregard what I will present in this book. After all, are you succeeding by other standards? Is there any room for improvement in your life?

Time-Tested

Time is a great tester, a great separator of the good from the bad. It ultimately illuminates which principles work and which principles don't. Biblical principles and values cannot be improved upon. My standing challenge is: Show me one valid principle that works whose roots are not in the Bible. I'm still waiting for the first response. With such a time-tested foundation, I do not hesitate to recommend biblical principles to help you reach your financial goals.

There are certain unalterable laws that must be followed by those attempting to develop a successful life. The truth of these laws does not depend on man's acceptance of them. The fact that gravity works is true whether you believe it or not. Just jump off a ten-story building and see. Violate this law and you will pay the consequences. The law of gravity is no respecter of persons, nor are the laws of sound financial judgement.

I will have been well paid, if, in some small way, I can help rekindle in you the values and ethical principles that are so important to our families, businesses, nation, and the world.

The Bottom Line

One of the most brilliant minds in history gives us the bottom line in a single sentence: *"Be not deceived; God is not mocked: for whatsoever a man soweth, that shall he also reap"* (Paul, Galatians 6:7—KJV). Good, sound, healthy financial seed will produce a healthy financial harvest. Bad, ill-advised seed will produce disaster. In fact, you will reap *more* than you sow in either case, because seeds always multiply. Right and timely decisions make for right and timely results. Bad and untimely decisions create a recipe for disaster.

Money does grow on trees, but you must understand the principles that make your money tree flourish.

---

*Those who fail can tell you what is
wrong with everyone else.*

CHAPTER TWO

Checkup Time

Dishonest money dwindles away,
but he who gathers money little by little
makes it grow.
— Proverbs 13:11

A thorough inspection is a must for your money tree. How are you doing financially? Are your current needs being met? Are you saving for those inevitable "rainy" days ahead? Do you have a plan for paying for your children's education? Where will you be financially when retirement years come? Will you have adequate resources to maintain a reasonable standard of living, or will you be a ward of the state or a financial burden on your children? These are questions that too few consider until it is too late.

To the young, retirement is light years away. As far as saving for near-term needs, most don't have a clue as to what their near-term needs are.

"Rainy day! What's that? Everything is bright and sunny and I have too many things to enjoy to be worried about a rainy day sometime in the future. Retirement? We've barely gotten started in life; we have plenty of time for that."

The middle-aged couple, busy raising a family, thinks the clock is still at high noon and that there is plenty of time .. well, maybe!

Prepared or not, we most likely will have near-term emergencies, and unless we die early, we *will* live into our retirement years. Whether we like it or not, we will be called upon to make many decisions that will affect our financial well-being. The decisions we make early in life will make a vast difference as to whether we become dependent or independent financially.

The End of the Rainbow

The vast majority of the elderly will find no pot of gold for their golden years at the end of the rainbow—only a sackful of lead.

We are told that 80 percent of today's retirees live below the poverty level. Fifteen percent live barely above the line and only 5 percent are financially independent. This is shocking news indeed, especially in view of the fact that the Social Security system may be in trouble.

Inflation will continue to eat at the value of the dollar. The continuing high cost of health care and the increase in life expectancy will put an additional burden on everyone. There are approximately thirty million people over the age of sixty-five in the United States. The fastest-growing segment of the population is eighty-five and over. Add to this the diminishing percentage of young people coming into the work force, and the problem multiplies. The Social Security system is dependent on new workers coming into the work force to pay benefits to the older folks. The system may not even survive.

Trouble Ahead

Serious trouble lies ahead. The government has already borrowed from the Social Security Funds to pay other debt.

Hopefully, you can see why it is more important than ever to start your financial planning in the early years. Those who plan to depend solely on Social Security may be in for a rude awakening. Ask those living on Social Security today how far their checks go.

So what is the solution? How do I become financially secure and prepared for whatever crisis comes along? How do I prepare now for my retirement years? How do I avoid becoming a burden to my children and society?

No Guarantees

Life offers no guarantees. It is uncertain at best. Disaster and the unexpected lurk all around us.

Nothing is sure in this life except "death and taxes," and some even try to beat those. Our jails are full of those who thought they could outsmart the IRS. For those who try to beat death, a whole new business has sprung up: people are frozen at death and stored in an ice vault. These people hope to be thawed out in some future millennium when science discovers a cure for disease and old age. That is a mighty long time to have a "cold head"!

In the midst of all these uncertainties, we are wise to make preparation and provision for the present and for the future. Making no preparation can mean disaster at any stage along the way.

The laws and principles that I shall outline, if followed, will save you many a sleepless night, numerous relationships, and perhaps even your marriage. If you expect to have a secure retirement, you must begin right now! Procrastination is a thief!

It's Your Choice

There are three basic rules to follow if you desire financial security and want to eliminate your major debt load:

- You must want to.
- You must plan to.
- You must work the plan and discipline yourself to hang in there.

It's up to you!

There are many voices that call you down dead-end streets and detour you from your goals. It is easy to let the circumstances of life rule over you and cause you to drown in a mass of financial entanglements. It takes little effort to float down the river with the current, but it takes a lot of energy to paddle upstream. No battle has ever been won floating down "easy river." Even dead fish can float downstream; but it takes a strong one to swim upstream. The goodies belong to those who prepare themselves, are on the offensive, and follow the rules that have been proven to work.

---

*Finish your outdoor work and get
your fields ready;
after that, build your house.*
— Proverbs 24:27

CHAPTER THREE

Money, What Is It?

One man pretends to be rich, yet has nothing;
another pretends to be poor, yet has great wealth.
— Proverbs 13:7

Son: "Mom, how much am I worth to you?"
Mom: "You're worth a million dollars!"
Son: "In that case, could you advance me twenty-five?"

What is money? Money is like a man full of energy, a boiler full of steam, a tank full of gas—all are full of power. However, a man may get sick, a boiler may burst, a tank may spring a leak, and all may lose their power. Money must be under control, properly directed, and the on and off switch operational if it is to work for you.

Stored Energy

Simply stated, money is a means of storing, or "warehousing," energy. Stored energy in exchange for work—dollars traded for work. Goods and services bought with dollars are actually the exchange of someone else's labor for yours. Money, wealth, and assets are stored energy that someone had to sweat for.

Money in itself is neither good nor bad. How we spend it and use it determines its rightness or wrongness. We make the ultimate decisions to waste, give, hoard, or spend it. Making the right decisions involves proper money management and an understanding of money.

When we waste money or spend it foolishly, we waste our own energy or someone else's. Would we be so foolish, after a hard month of labor, to put all the money we earned into a stove and burn it? Yet this is an accurate picture of our waste!

Seeing money as energy explains one reason that theft is wrong. Stealing is taking stored-up energy in the form of dollars or valuable objects that someone else worked for—without giving energy in return.

Taken a step farther, you can see that poor performance on the job, laziness, and goofing off are the same as stealing energy. We are accepting dollars in pay (energy stored from someone else's labor) and giving no work or energy in return. Society cannot remain stable for long if the wagon becomes too loaded with such people. No one will be left to pull it.

The Biblical View

What you think the Bible teaches about money may not be exactly correct. The Bible teaches that "the *love* of money is a root of all kinds of evil" (1 Timothy 6:10, italics added). It does not teach that money in and of itself is evil. The root of evil is in the mind. The Bible talks about many wealthy men who pleased God. Their wealth did not possess them; they possessed their wealth. Their trust was in the giver, not the gift. Job, Abraham, Joseph, and Daniel are but a few examples.

There are many verses that teach it is wrong to hoard money or allow it to be our sole aim in life. Jesus said, *"Lay not up for yourselves treasures upon earth . . . but in heaven"* (Matthew 6:19-20—KJV). *"For what is a man profited, if he shall gain the whole world, and lose his own soul?"* (Matthew 16:26—KJV).

Jesus is not teaching against providing for our families or investing some of the blessings God has placed in our hands. He is talking about priorities and knowing what is truly valuable in life. Our priority should not be money, but the proper use of money. And we should ask ourselves where our trust lies—in God, our benevolent heavenly father, or in money.

There are many passages that command us to be good stewards (managers) and to invest and use our wealth in the right ways. The parable of the talents in Matthew 25:14-30 is one of many examples. In this parable, the steward who failed to wisely invest the money that God had entrusted him was condemned. The other two stewards were commended for the gain on their investments and the proper use of money placed in their hands.

The biblical view of wealth, therefore, teaches individual responsibility, work, and proper use of our money for the betterment of the world and our own families. Our nation was founded upon these principles.

You Can't Get Water From a Dry Well

Why is money management so important?

Do you own a house, farm, or business? Did you borrow money for your investment? How were you able to borrow those funds? The bank does not print money when it runs low; the bank loans dollars that other people have entrusted or loaned to it (energy), enabling you to borrow from this energy source. You, in turn, pay back the bank with energy (money) in order for that institution to be able to loan to someone else.

When you borrow money to build a house, the bank makes a profit. You use the money to make the investment and hope to someday sell it at a profit. The people that you bought the material from to build your house are in it to make a profit. You also provide jobs for those who build the house so that they can make money to loan to the bank to loan to others, and on and on it goes.

Money, properly used, simply provides a system whereby commerce can operate and be dependable. Everyone profits and society functions as it should. Our children and grandchildren's future is secure only when we properly manage our money to the betterment of, not only our families, but society in general.

Those who make a profit and succeed in business are a blessing to our nation. Each makes a contribution to society and expends his energy in a useful way. These people are conduits through which God showers his blessings upon mankind.

America has become the most prosperous nation in all the world because of this very principle. We call it capitalism. If you want to see the effect of the opposite system, where everything is taken away from the individual, where freedom is suppressed and creativity stifled, then take a look at the Soviet Empire, which is now experiencing great difficulty after a seventy-year experiment. Their factories are obsolete, their store shelves empty, their rivers polluted, and their future uncertain.

Of course, there are abusers and scoundrels in our system, but it has worked well and will continue to work as long as the majority understands these principles and invests its energy in our future. All of this combines to make a better financial world, not only for ourselves, but for those that follow after us.

Not in the clamor of the crowded street,
not in the shouts and plaudits of the throng.
But in ourselves are triumph and defeat.
— Longfellow

CHAPTER FOUR

The American Dream— Or Nightmare?

We may live on by effort and plan
When the fine bloom of living is shed.
But God pity the little that's left of a man
When the last of his dreams is dead.
— William Herbert Carruth

Dreams are the foundation of success, but we must keep our feet on the ground, at least a good part of the time. We have been so bombarded by TV, newspapers, and politicians about the American Dream that we have come to believe that we are owed success by society in general and the federal government in particular. As a result of this mentality, most of the younger generation enter adulthood expecting the impossible and then set out to get it.

The American Dream
The American Dream comes true at the early age of 24:
- A beautiful home—financed with a 30-year mortgage.
- Beautiful furniture—financed on a 48-month plan.
- Modern appliances—financed on a 48-month plan.

- Two cars—financed on two 48-month plans.
- Vacation cabin on the lake—financed with a 15-year mortgage.
- Boat and trailer—financed on a 48-month plan.
- Riding lawn mower—financed on a 36-month plan.
- A fur coat—financed on a 36-month plan.
- A handful of credit cards available to buy gas and lodging for the annual credit-card vacation.

There you have it! Now for the next thirty years, all your dreams will become a nightmare as you try to figure out how to meet all these monthly payments, not to mention your general living expenses.

Well, no problem. The macho, John Wayne mentality can cope with any battle and win! (He hasn't lost one yet, right?)

The American Nightmare

Multitudes enter their adult years, where real responsibility is required, without any money-management skills. Many times they are not even able to balance their checkbook. They have easy access to credit cards and a multitude of businesses willing to sell to them on credit. Armed with such "easy" credit, millions swim unawares into shark-infested waters. They have money to spend, and a million hands reach out to claim it. For so many, the American Dream is a mirage and quickly turns into a nightmare·

Dreams *Can* Come True

As Americans, we are blessed, and many of our dreams can come true provided we properly manage our time and wealth. There are millions around the world that would give anything to have the chance in life that we Americans take for granted.

Before the pilgrims ever set sail for the new world, their hearts were fired with the dream of freedom. Never underestimate the power of dreams. You must see it in your mind and dream it in your heart before you can actually accomplish your goal.

You must also be flexible and know when to let go of a dream. When you discover that a dream is impossible to accomplish, it's time to find another one. It's okay to hitch your wagon to a star, but be sure you know how to unhitch it before it falls.

Fact is, when your ship finally comes in,
all of your relatives will be waiting at the dock.

SECTION II

The Branches of Your Money Tree

CHAPTER FIVE

Faith

*Now faith is being sure of what we hope for
and certain of what we do not see.*
— Hebrews 11:1

The fifteen "branches" in this section may seem somewhat disconnected with making money grow on trees, but let me assure you that they are vital.

Yes, there are success stories where some of these branches have been ignored. But true success is not measured in dollars alone.

I will be discussing not just money, but relationships, purpose, and moral values—essential foundation blocks of a truly successful life and a productive money tree. Your money tree will surely grow and flourish if these fifteen branches are cultivated and developed throughout your lifetime.

The first branch, faith, sets the direction and lays the foundation for a successful life and prosperous money tree. You need a strong faith branch because our world is filled with uncertainties, danger, distrust, and disappointment. A healthy faith branch will enable you to keep believing that you will reap a good harvest by planting good seed. The faith anchor will stay the course when the storms come.

Two Grains of Corn

Once upon a time there were two grains of corn. One day they were discussing their future, and a farmer friend overheard their conversation.

"Your future," said the farmer, "is only secure if you put your faith in me. I will take you from this warm, dry, secure barn and bury you in a dark hole, where it is cold and wet in the winter and hot and dry in the summer. After several days, you will die and your bodies will decay and become part of the earth's soil.

"There is something in you that no one can see. As you die, it will push very hard and break through the packed earth. At first, it will look like a blade of grass, but soon it will grow tall and have blooms at its top. Small shoots like ears will push outward from its side and grow big, until they are filled with hundreds of beautiful golden grains just like you. This is the only way to insure your future."

One grain said, "The farmer is a good and kind man. I will trust him, even though I do not understand and am afraid. I will let him do with me as he has said."

The other grain said, "No. I'm happy and content to live here in this warm, dry barn, away from the winter cold and the summer heat. I want to live here in security and comfort." So each grain of corn did as it had said.

One day a hungry rat ran through the barn and saw the beautiful, yellow grain of corn sleeping in his warm bed. Being extremely hungry, the rat grabbed the grain of corn and ate it very quickly.

The grain that was planted by the kind farmer also died; but just as the farmer promised, soon there were hundreds of beautiful grains of corn in its place.

One grain became a meal for a single hungry rat. The other grain is still feeding thousands of hungry animals and people all over the world—and its children are countless.

Faith in the farmer made all the difference.

Mans' Desire to Excel

Created within us is an unquenchable thirst to know, understand, explore, and reach up.

We ask questions such as: Who am I? Where did I come from? Where am I going? Why am I here?

Man's search for answers and his desire to excel never ends. The painter is always working on his masterpiece; the doctor, on the cure for some dreaded disease; the architect, on the perfect plan; the businessman, for record sales and profits.

We put a man on the moon, and now we want to explore distant planets. We send out spaceships that travel past galaxies into limitless space. We spend billions of dollars on giant telescopes and launch them into space in order to get a peek at our universe. We send out highly-sophisticated listening devices, hoping to hear a sound of life in some distant galaxy.

The desire to know and to accomplish is good and places man on a level far above any other earthly creature. All is well and good as long as this ambition is under control and put into proper perspective.

Why Do We Fail?

With all of man's drive and search for knowledge, we are still unable to live peacefully on our own planet. With all the massive resources at our disposal, we fail to reach attainable goals. Why?

The answer lies in the fact that man can reach the zenith only when the inward part—the heart—is ruled by divine power. God, our creator, the master architect, surely knows his own creation and how we can reach our potential. He knows how to direct us toward the betterment of all his creation, to his glory.

The Basis of Faith

I am a believer in God. My conviction is not based on what is sometimes called "blind faith," but on a faith that is founded on evidence. Where there is design, there has to be a designer. Where there is order, there must be an "order-maker." Where there are "natural laws," there must be a lawgiver.

This world is made up of life and matter. Either lifeless matter has always existed; or God, the creator of life, has always existed. If only matter has always existed, then out of dead, lifeless matter sprang life. If God has always existed, then from an intelligent being, life and all its complexities were created. Our sun is just one medium-sized star in our galaxy of 100 billion other stars. Our galaxy being just one of an estimated 100 billion other galaxies, each with their 100 billion stars. Little wonder the Psalmist was inspired to write, "The heavens declare the glory of God. The skies proclaim the work of his hands" (Psalms 19:1). All evidence points to the fact that thought, design, and awesome power created our universe.

Another evidence that gives me faith is the resurrection—the empty tomb. This event defies explanation. It could have been nothing less than a miracle. The resurrection is the linchpen of faith. From death to life, dead men will live again!

The choice for me is not difficult. This belief and confidence in a divine creator is called "faith."

The Value of God's Laws

Just as our universe is governed by order and design, we, too, live under law and order. We have purpose and are responsible creatures. Punishment must be administered for violations of moral, as well as civil, law. Otherwise, society could not exist in any orderly form. Chaos would reign. The law of the jungle would rule—the stronger controlling the weaker—might makes right. If there is no supreme law of right and wrong, no unchangeable moral standards, then who is to be the judge of right and wrong? My rights are just as right as your rights. Who tells me if it's wrong to kill, steal, or lie? Who can be judge over these matters?

Our nation was founded upon the concept of a divine creator and lawgiver. Under this concept, our nation has flourished like no other nation in history. If you want to see a society that followed the other philosophy—that is, that God does not exist—then you have only to take a look at the Soviet Union.

The Benefits of Faith

How does all this relate to my money tree? By living under the canopy of the moral laws and concepts given by our creator, society can function and flourish in an orderly fashion. Rights are protected, and the weak and helpless are cared for. In such an atmosphere, freedom flourishes, creativity is encouraged, our factories and institutions operate efficiently, investments are safe, and our people prosper.

In nations where the concepts of faith and morality are restricted, freedom, human progress, wealth, and peace are also restricted. Civilizations who have trampled these principles underfoot now lie in ruin.

When we speak of faith, we generally think of faith in God. However, faith in our fellowman is also important. Trust and respect are vital when dealing with our families, friends, employers, employees, and customers. A society in which there is no trust will not prosper. Faith, not only in God but in our fellow man, breeds eternal hope and trust.

Faith, hope, and trust are indispensable ingredients for success. Without them, your money tree will wither and die. Let your roots go deep to nourish your most important branch—faith. For it is the foundation of your money tree.

You may lose your wealth and your health,
but never lose your survival kit:
faith, hope and trust.

CHAPTER SIX

Attitude

*He that is of a merry heart
hath a continual feast.*
— Proverbs 15:15 (KJV)

Look out! Your attitude is showing. Our attitude plays a major role in our success or failure.

Vachel Lindsey, the poet, told of an experience he had one night. He was tired and hungry, so he stopped at a farmhouse and asked to spend the night. He had no money, but offered to pay for lodging by reciting original poetry. The lady of the house was not interested in poetry and pointed him to a small house across the field. When he reached the little house, he was invited in and told he could stay if he could accept the meager surroundings. There were only two small rooms. There were no window shades and no rugs on the floor. The only furniture was a sagging bed, a rickety table, an old stove, and two broken-down chairs.

When Lindsey left the next morning, he told a friend, "That man had nothing and gave me half of it, and we both had abundance."

Lindsey could have complained about the run-down shack he was forced to spend the night in or about how

31

he wasted his time reciting poetry to such an ignorant country bumkin. What made his outlook different? Attitude. He came away with a blessing.

Life, to a large degree, is how we view it. When you look at a rosebush, do you see beautiful roses or do you see prickly thorns?

Your outlook determines your outcome. Do you view obstacles as opportunities or as brick walls? As it has been said, "One person looked through bars and saw mud. Another looked through bars and saw stars." Our focus determines to a large degree what we see.

Attitude Is a Choice

It is a known fact that production in a factory is often higher on Friday, simply because the end of the work week is near and attitudes have changed. Our attitude shows in our faces, our work, and our conversation.

Daddy's Store

One day in Chicago's new Marshall Field's Department Store, Mr. Field was walking the aisles and observing his customers. He overheard a little girl telling her friend how her daddy ran one of the departments in the store. She talked on and on about "daddy's store" and "daddy's department," as if he owned it. Suddenly, her mother recognized Mr. Field standing in the aisle listening to the little girl's conversation and, of course, was very embarrassed. She began to apologize for her daughter's statements, but Mr. Field stopped her and said, "The little girl is right. I want her father to feel it is his store and his department. If I could induce every employee to have this attitude, I wouldn't have to be concerned about the success of this business."

Well put, Mr. Field. People who develop such attitudes about their jobs will not be overlooked at promotion or pay-raise time. The world is starving for people with positive, wholesome attitudes.

The Farmer and the Thorn Tree

There was a farmer who always had a smile and good things to say about even the worst circumstances in life. The neighbors thought surely there must be something that would make "John" lose his head and complain, so they were always on the alert to catch him in such a moment.

One day, John bought a big bull at the stockyards; but unbeknownst to him, the bull was extremely vicious. The neighbors all learned about the big, mean bull and gathered at John's farm the day it was to be delivered.

John stood in the middle of the pasture with a bucketful of feed, beckoning the bull to get out of the cattle truck. Sure enough, the bull bolted out, snorting and pawing, and headed straight for John. There was no time to get out of the pasture. John knew he was in deep trouble. The bull, still snorting, ran toward him with head twisting and horns flashing. There was a tall thorn tree nearby, and his only chance was to climb that tree. Climb it he did, to the very top, out of the bull's reach.

The neighbors just rolled in laughter. They knew they had John this time. There was no way to make a good thing out of this ordeal. Finally, after the bull had been chased away, John came down from the thorn tree, bleeding from head to toe. His hands were full of thorns, his clothes were torn, and he was barely able to walk.

"Well John," the neighbors said, "how is the day going, and what have you got to say about all this?"

John replied, "Wow! What a fantastic view! Never before have I had the opportunity to get such a view of my farm."

So it is. We see what we want to see, and this makes all the difference in our attitude.

The Lazy Bum

A man passing through a small community saw a shabbily-dressed man near a run-down shack. The man was hoeing his grass-infested garden while sitting in an old, broken-down chair. The passerby immediately decided that the shabby man was a shiftless, lazy bum. As he drove around the bend, he looked back and was able to see the man from another angle. What he saw brought a lump to his throat. He had made a tragic mistake. He now could see two empty pant legs draped over the man's lap, and he could see that the chair was a wheelchair.

So it is with us. We sometimes see only a small part of the whole, and this affects our entire attitude.

"Well, That's Different!"

The story is told about a woman in a Boston hotel who complained to the manager that the guest in the next room pounded on the piano all day long. The woman was ready to scream. The hotel manager said, "Dear lady, I would like to help you, but I wouldn't dare. You see, he is rehearsing for his concert tonight, his name is Paderewski."

The woman replied, "Really? Well, that's different."

Then for the next several minutes she called all her friends and invited them to her room to listen to the famous pianist.

What a rapid recovery she had!

Wearing Blinders

As a young boy, I would watch Papa put blinders on the mule and hitch him to the plow. The blinders limited the mule's side vision and kept him from being distracted as he plowed between the rows of corn. But, it is not too wise for human beings to wear blinders. Too many of us do wear blinders and can see only in one direction. Thus, we form attitudes based on incorrect information.

Be sure you tend carefully to your attitude branch, as it easily becomes full of rotten fruit. Water and prune it often, so you can have a good view of everything that surrounds you.

A cheerful look brings joy to the heart,
and good news gives health to the bones.
— Proverbs 15:30

CHAPTER SEVEN

Honesty

Honest scales and balances are from the Lord.
— Proverbs 16:11

"Honesty Is the Best Policy"

Probably no man has ever had a longer or more distinguished sports career than coach Amos Alonzo Stagg, who for forty-two years served at the University of Chicago.

On one occasion when Coach Stagg's champion baseball team was defending its title, the batter hit a single, and one of Staggs' players was headed home with the winning run. Stagg shouted, "Get back to third base! You cut it by a yard!" The runner replied, "But the umpire didn't see me!" Stagg shouted, "That doesn't make any difference! Get back!" They lost the game, but a character battle was won.

"Honesty is the best policy." It may sound old-fashioned and simple, but it is still true. No matter what the profession or business, integrity is indispensable.

There are many shortcuts along life's pathway, and you may even reach your desired destination by taking a few. However, there are no shortcuts to honesty and integrity.

It's a Deal

In my fifty years of business experience, dealing with thousands of situations, I can attest to the fact that there has been a shocking decline in honesty and integrity. No longer are a handshake and a person's word always reliable. This is alarming indeed when you consider that the American system of free enterprise and its institutions were built on and have flourished on trust and integrity.

Billions of dollars change hands everyday on pieces of paper; billions of dollars worth of merchandise is shipped from our factories and farms on credit, with only an invoice and a promise to pay. The manufacturer (producer), the distributor (retailer), and the buyer (consumer) are all interlocked, and credibility is essential to success. Every job in America is somehow directly or indirectly affected by this system of faith and trust. Yet, so many are dishonest. Our free enterprise, market-driven system is weakened with each dishonest act.

Theft

It is extremely important to teach our children ethical and moral values from their earliest years. Children that grow up seeing dishonesty will follow by example. Shoplifting (stealing) by customers and theft by employees has soared. A retail company with sales of $100 million will lose up to $5 million annually through shoplifting. This does not include the cost of security guards and systems used to prevent theft. Who pays for all this? The consumer ultimately has to pay. Every time you make a purchase, you pay for these losses in higher prices.

I know of and have witnessed many sad situations in which respected, well-off people were caught shoplifting. Some mothers actually teach their small children the art of stealing. The crime occurs in every strata of society, rich and poor. In my companies I have been robbed many times. One manager was shot and killed and millions of dollars have been lost to thieves.

I can count on my fingers the times someone has volunteered to make restitution for a theft. This does happen, however, and when it does, it helps restore faith in your fellow man.

It Does Happen

On one occasion, I received a letter from a young man in the Army with a check for $3,000. I almost fell out of my chair. The young soldier told me he had stolen things from one of our stores in Alabama while an employee there. He had since become a Christian and was intent on restoring what he had taken.

Another incident stands out in my mind. A young woman who had taken a few small things while working in another of our stores also sent me a check. Included in her calculation of what she owed was interest that dated from the time she had taken the merchandise.

Honesty Pays

Now what does all this mean for my money tree? Just this: businesses of all kinds are looking for talented, hard-working, honest employees. Just as surely as the sun rises, honest people will rise to the top. The future is bright and wide open for good, honest, credible people. The jobs of industry and commerce are crying for quality people. What bank, retail store, factory, or office does not prefer an honest person?

No matter what field of business or profession you enter, honesty and integrity are indispensable. Few will ever reach the top without them; and those few who do will not remain there for long. In spite of the bad publicity of some, a large percentage of those at the top of big companies are men and women of integrity and traditional values—people you can trust and depend on. Integrity, in the long run, will always win out over cleverness and manipulation.

"A good name is more desirable than great riches; to be esteemed is better than silver or gold" (Proverbs 22:1).

Not As Good As They Look

There is a story about an advertising man who worked for John Wanamaker, the department store tycoon. This man always told the truth. Even in the advertisements he wrote, he endeavored to tell only the truth. One day he was to write up an ad for some neckties at a bargain price of 25 cents each—quite a bargain, even in those days. After examining the ties, he found that some were of second-rate quality and hesitated to advertise them even at the 25-cent special.

After considerable thought, he sat down and made up the ad with the following headline:

"They are not as good as they look, but they are good enough—25¢."

The store was rushed, and they did not have enough ties to fill the demand. In fact, they had to keep buying the cheap ties to satisfy all the customers.

Truth sometimes hurts, but in the long run it is best. When you tell the truth and are completely honest, you never have to remember what you said if you are called upon to repeat it. What the world needs is fewer wishbones, jawbones, and knucklebones and a whole lot more backbones.

Nourish this branch of your money tree at all costs, and it will increase your deposits. Honesty is still the best policy.

Kings take pleasure in honest lips;
they value a man who speaks the truth.
— Proverbs 16:13

CHAPTER EIGHT

Communication

The more the words, the less the meaning,
and how does that profit anyone?
— Ecclesiastes 6:11

An after-dinner speaker was waxing bold while rattling off a long list of statistics. He summed up by saying, "These are not my own figures; they are the figures of someone who knows what he is talking about."

Good communication is vital to your money tree. You must be able to communicate properly to get things done and to avoid conflict and heartache. Countless arguments, mistakes, nervous breakdowns, and even wars could be avoided through better communication.

The lack of good communication slowly eats away at relationships and creates suspicion and doubt. We must learn to share ideas and thoughts with our associates and family if we expect to maintain relationships that are fruitful. The closer the relationship, the more important it is that the lines of communication stay open.

Communication is a two-way street. We often lecture when we should be listening. Listening is one of the surest ways to determine if your message is getting through.

Getting the Whole Story

It's dangerous to draw conclusions before you have all the facts. Many times, if you will just wait, you will find out that what you are hearing is not what is being said. A classic example of this is a story from the historic battle between Wellington and Napoleon.

It was June 18, 1815, the Battle of Waterloo. The French, under the command of Napoleon, were fighting the Allies (British, Dutch, and German) under the command of Wellington. The people of England depended on a system of semaphore signals to find out how the battle was going. One of these signal stations was on the tower of Winchester Cathedral.

Late in the day it flashed the signal: "W-E-L-L-I-N-G-T-O-N—D-E-F-E-A-T-E-D—." Just at that moment one of those sudden English fog clouds made it impossible to read the message. The news of defeat quickly spread throughout the city. The whole countryside was sad and gloomy when they heard the news that their country had lost the war. Suddenly the fog lifted, and the remainder of the message could be read. The message had four words, not two. The complete message was: "W-E-L-L-I-N-G-T-O-N—D-E-F-E-A-T-E-D—-T-H-E—E-N-E-M-Y!" It took only a few minutes for the good news to spread. Sorrow was turned into joy, defeat was turned into victory!

Bring Your Wife, "Gas"

Having all the facts is essential if you are to be credible in your communication. Some of those "personal" computer letters are glaringly inaccurate.

Occasionally, I get one to "Mr. and Mrs. Howard Publishing." I also have a firm by the name of Lakeland Oil & Gas. Are you ready for this one?

```
        Congratulations Mr. and Mrs. Lakeland
                 Oil and Gas!

Dear Lakeland Oil and Gas,
    You have been personally selected to
receive a free all-expense paid vacation to
Florida and a free motor boat simply by
visiting our beautiful resort. You will
enjoy the beautiful sandy beaches and the
blue waters of the gulf. . . .
    Mr. Oil, in order to qualify, you must
also bring along your wife, Gas, as the
reservations are for the both of you. . ."
```

(By the way, the "motor boat" was a rubber raft with a plastic, battery-powered propeller.)

No doubt about it, improper communication is one of the most serious problems in both business and personal relationships.

No Pencils

A little boy said to his teacher, "I ain't got no pencil." She corrected him, "It's 'I don't have a pencil, you don't have a pencil, we don't have pencils, and they don't have pencils.' Is that clear?"

"No ma'am," said the puzzled little boy. "What happened to all them pencils?"

Well, He Tried

A teacher had no problem in understanding this telephone conversation:

Voice: "Ronald Jones is sick and won't be in school today."

Teacher: "Who is speaking, please?"

Voice: "This is my father."

Just Trying To Do My Job

This next story was given to me by an associate. While I'll not vouch that it actually happened, it does demonstrate a valuable communication skill.

```
To Whom It May Concern:
     I am writing in response to your request
for additional information. In Block No. 3 of
the accident report form, I put "trying to do
the job alone" as the cause of my accident.
     You said in your letter that I should
explain more fully, and I trust the following
details will be sufficient.
     I am a brick layer by trade. On the date
of the accident, I was working alone on the
roof of a new six-story office building.
```

When I had completed my work, I discovered that I had approximately 500 pounds of brick left over. Rather than carry the bricks down by hand, I decided to lower the bricks down in a barrel by using a pulley that was attached to the top of the building.

Securing the rope at ground level, I went up to the roof, swung the barrel out, and proceeded to load the brick into it. Then I went back to the ground and untied the rope, holding it tightly to insure a slow descent of the 500 pounds of brick. (Now you will note in Block No. 2 of the accident report form that I weigh 135 pounds.)

Due to my surprise at being jerked off the ground so suddenly, I lost my presence of mind and forgot to let go of the rope. Needless to say, I proceeded at a rather rapid rate up the side of the building. In the vicinity of the third floor, I met the barrel coming down. This explains the fractured skull and broken collarbone. Slowed only slightly, I continued my rapid ascent, not stopping until the fingers of my right hand were two knuckles deep into the pulley.

Fortunately, however, by this time I had regained my presence of mind and was able to hold tightly to the rope in spite of my pain. At approximately the same time, however, the barrel of bricks hit the ground and the bottom fell out of the barrel. Devoid of the weight of the bricks, the barrel weighs approximately 50 pounds. (I again refer you to my weight in Block No. 2.)

As you might imagine, I began a rather rapid descent down the side of the building. In the vicinity of the third floor, I again met the barrel coming up. This accounts for the two broken ankles and the lacerations on my legs and lower body.

The encounter with the barrel slowed me enough to lessen my injuries. Fortunately, only three vertebrae were cracked when I fell on the bricks.

I am sorry to report, however, that as I lay there on the bricks in pain, unable to stand, and watching the empty barrel six

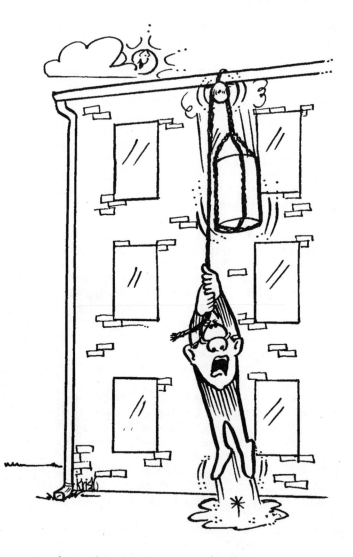

stories above me, I again lost my presence of mind and let go of the rope.

The empty barrel weighed more than the rope, and it came down on me and broke both my legs.

I hope that I have furnished enough information as to how the accident occurred. Because, you see, I was trying to do the job alone.

Sincerely,

This story uses one of the best forms of communication. Not only do you have a blow-by-blow description of what is happening, but you can visualize in your mind the poor fellow going up and down the side of the building and the barrel and bricks doing him great bodily harm.

This is the same principle that Jesus, the master communicator, used in his parables and stories.

"Behold a sower went forth to sow . . ."

"There was a certain man that had two sons . . ."

"The lost sheep . . . the lost coin . . ."

"The Good Samaritan . . ." and many others.

"I'm Gonna Get You"

Another strong way to communicate is with the skillful use of punishment and reward. Parents use these techniques quite often. A mother asks, "Johnny, do you want me to knock your head off?" Well, of course the "little rascal" doesn't. So he complies. Sometimes, however, it doesn't work!

Again, same mother, same "little rascal." "Now, Johnny, if you do that one more time, I'm going to kill you!" Really? Has Johnny ever seen Mom kill anyone? Not likely.

Again, same mother, same "little rascal." "Now, Johnny, for the fifth and final time. This is it. I'm going to count to ten. If you don't stop that, I'm going to beat the tar out of you!" Well, it's doubtful that little Johnny has ever seen the "tar" beaten out of anyone by Mom.

One more try. Same mother, same "little rascal." "Now, Jonathan, I'm going to tell your Dad when he gets home, and you know what that means." That did it. Johnny now knows he's in big trouble. He got the point.

Her communication was excellent. The problem was that Johnny simply didn't believe a word of what she said until the end. Why? Because Mom had communicated to him many times before that no action would be taken. He understood her perfectly. But in the final scenario, he knew he was in deep trouble because of past experiences with his father.

Here We Go Again

Three-year-old Bobby was being a "little devil" in church. On this particular Sunday morning, his daddy finally had enough. He grabbed Bobby, threw him across his shoulder, and headed for the back door. Little Bobby knew exactly what he was in for. As they were almost out of the auditorium, little Bobby, with all the

urgency he could muster, yelled back to the congregation, "Here we go again! Ya'll please pray for me!" A perfect little communicator.

Actions Speak Louder Than Words

One area of communication that we may overlook is our body language. Experts say there are hundreds upon hundreds of movements that constitute body language: raised eyebrows, a shrug of the shoulders, hand gestures, a puzzled look, a nod of approval, a yawn. These are but a few of the hundreds of ways we communicate without saying a word.

A whole new science has developed in the art of negotiations that involves body language. Studies show that non-verbal body language carries 65 percent of the message. Are your hands clasped together? Are you leaning back in your chair, folding your arms across your chest, fidgeting with paper, thumping the desk, or twisting and turning? Even your choice of seating at a table conveys messages. There are dozens of body signals that tell the opposition how you are responding and give valuable clues to your real position in the negotiations. In fact, you can give away your deal without ever opening your mouth if the opposition knows how to read and interpret your body signs.

Too Much Communication Can Go Wrong

A man accused of purse snatching decided to act as his own attorney in court. In cross examination of the victim, he concluded with this final question: "Did you get a good look at my face when I snatched your purse?"

He got ten years.

Expert Communication Skills

Mrs. Smith wanted to publish a book on her family roots, so she hired a professional writer to research and write the book.

After a few months of research, the writer advised Mrs. Smith that he had discovered some unpleasant and disturbing facts.

It seemed that Great-Great Grandfather John Smith had been a notorious bank robber, had murdered several men in pursuit of this trade, and had been sentenced to die in the state's electric chair. The writer wanted Mrs. Smith to advise him as to how he should handle this bit of disgraceful news.

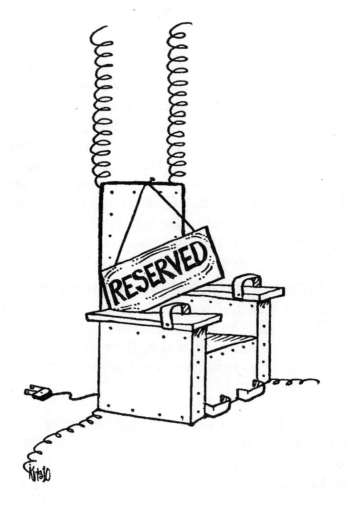

Mrs. Smith, wanting to protect her good name, yet wanting to be truthful, asked the writer to dress up the facts about "Grandpaw" and put them in the best light possible. The following story appeared under the John Smith branch of the family tree:

> John Smith, son of Samuel and Josephine Smith, was born July 2, 1892, and rose to fame at the early age of thirty-seven.
>
> He was elected by his peers to a seat in one of the respected institutions of his state, where he was to pursue an electrifying career. This occasion received national attention, and the entire press corps gave special coverage to the proceedings.
>
> While there, he occupied a chair reserved especially for him in which no other person felt qualified to sit. However, because of the intensity of the position in which he sat, he died very suddenly on the 3rd day of May, 1931, at 10:05 A.M., thus bringing to an end his widely acclaimed career.

"Sell" Your Idea

A good communicator is nothing more than a master salesman. Follow these basic communication principles to "sell" your ideas.

- You must know your product. You can't sell your idea or product if you don't know where the "hot button" is. The only thing you will communicate when you don't know what you are talking about is exactly that!

- You must believe in your product. Enthusiasm is catching, if you don't believe it, no one else will either. The story is told about the noted philosopher and agnostic, David Hume, who had been noticed attending the great reformer George Whitefield's revivals. On one occasion on his way to hear Whitefield, Hume was asked if he was beginning to believe what Whitefield was preaching. He answered that he was not, but that Whitefield believed what he preached so intensely that he just couldn't stay away.

• You must know your audience (customer). Be sure that you communicate on your audience's level. Never assume that another person understands even the simplest things. Many able, knowledgeable people "shoot" over their audience's head. It's like firing a blank cartridge: it makes a lot of noise, but brings home no bacon. You must also know the needs of your audience and how your product or idea can benefit them and improve their life. You must be able to zero in on your audience in order to make your sale.

• You must know how to "dress up your product." The buyer must be able to "try it on." This is why department stores have dressing rooms and full-length mirrors. The buyer must be able to "taste" your product. (You can't walk out of a ice cream store after a taste sample without a cone in your hand.)

You have got to sell the sizzle along with the steak. Sorry McDonalds, but the best hamburgers I ever ate were back at the ol' country fairs. No one had to say a word or twist my arm. All it took to convince me was a whiff floating on the breeze. Like a magnet, it would draw me to the hamburger tent. They always cooked the hamburgers on a hot griddle out in plain view. What an aroma! I could have eaten a dozen without one sales pitch. The message was effectively communicated to my stomach. The only trouble was, I only had one dime and could only buy one hamburger. (That's right, hamburgers only cost 10 cents back then.) Those ol' boys knew how to get the message out. They didn't need a canned commercial, just plain ol' temptation!

A good communicator will take the wraps off, and let you see it, feel it, and taste it. A communicator is just the back drop to highlight the merchandise (idea).

- You must know how and when to close the sale—when to get up, speak up, and shut up. A good communicator knows when to hand the customer a pen so he can sign on the dotted line. I don't know how many times I have seen a salesman talk himself out of a sale or a speech maker lose his audience because he didn't know how to close.

The old saying that you can lead a horse to water but you can't make him drink is not in a good communicator's vocabulary. A good communicator knows how to lead the horse to the water and when it's time to *allow* him to drink.

Twelve Rules of Good Communication
1. Have a stated purpose.
2. Know your subject.
3. Speak to the level of the audience.
4. Be concise—do not ramble.
5. Show confidence—believe in what you are saying.
6. Draw a word picture. Help your listeners see as well as hear.
7. Explain the benefits. What are the rewards?
8. Maintain good eye contact.
9. Be natural—don't use a "canned" approach.
10. Be consistent in your own life.
11. Eliminate all distractions.
12. Dress in keeping with the occasion.

Talk to your communication branch often. Master this one and you will never have to worry about withdrawal pains in your savings account.

We all are given two ends—
one for thinking, one for sitting.
Heads you win; tails you lose.

CHAPTER NINE

Time

There is a time for everything,
and a season for every activity under heaven.
— Ecclesiastes 3:1

One Strike and You're Out

The storm had battered the ship and it was going down. There was another ship nearby, but in the pitch-black darkness, no one could see the sinking ship.

One, lone, dry match was found, but who would strike it? The wind was blowing, and this one match was their only chance. Nervously, they waited; who would volunteer to strike the match? Seconds ticked away. Soon they reached a point when it was now or never. The other ship was drifting out of range, and with it, all hope of being sighted would be gone.

The passengers all gathered in a circle to shield the match from the wind. Finally, one man took the match and knelt down. Cupping his hands, he struck the match. Every eye was focused on the flickering match, and all the passengers held their breath. One flicker, then another—the match almost went out. The tiny flickering flame was held to the lantern's wick. All their hope was focused on that tiny flicker of light. The wick caught, light burst forth, and a cheer from the passengers went up. The rescue ship could now see the small lantern burning, and all the passengers were saved.

You see, time would not wait. At that particular point, an extra second would have meant that the opportunity had passed forever. The match would then have been useless.

So it is many times in life. Time will not wait. We have only a second to act, or it will pass—never to return.

The Mystery of Time

You may be able to make a hamburger or even an atomic bomb, but you cannot make time. Time is a gift from God and is very precious. How we use it makes a vast difference in our financial welfare, happiness, relationships, and every facet of our lives. You can waste it and ignore it, but you can't stop it. Your clock may lose time, gain time, or stop, but time itself is not affected.

Time towers over our every move and breath.

The doctor checks your heartbeat by it. You go to work, you go to bed, you get up, you go to church, you eat, and you travel by it. All commerce operates under time's watchful eye. Parliaments open and close with its permission. Wars begin and end; the grave opens to take our dead because of its vigil. Billions of documents are dated every day at time's bidding.

No one has ever been able to totally comprehend time. We can only segment it into seconds, minutes, hours, and years. But where time goes and from whence it came is a mystery that only God knows!

Time has enabled me to write these lines, the press to print them, the binder to bind them, the freight carrier to transport them, and you to read them.

You May Rob a Bank,
But You Can't Rob Time

How can I best use time to accomplish the most in life? Many businesses hire experts to make a time and motion study of their company. We hired such experts to make a study of our company. It cost over $100,000, and it was worth every cent.

The average business gets only 65 percent of the potential output from its employees. This is one of the reasons America has lost much of its competitive edge in world markets. The proper use of time is a key factor in whether we as a nation will survive in a new, competitive world. If we lose this battle, it will affect every American. We cannot rob time and get away with it. We will only rob ourselves. Time will not compromise to meet our standards.

Scheduling—How to Get More Out of Time

Charles Schwab, the famous steel king, was having trouble with efficiency in his steel plant, so he called in Ivy Lee, an efficiency expert, to show him how to run his company more efficiently.

Lee gave Schwab a piece of paper and told him to list the six most important things he had to do tomorrow.

After Schwab made his list, Lee then told him to number the tasks according to their importance and put the list in his pocket. The first thing in the morning, Schwab was to pull it out and start working on the tasks in numerical order. "Do this every day," advised Lee, "and when you are convinced of its value, send me a check for whatever you think it is worth." In a few weeks, Charles Schwab sent Lee a check for $25,000 along with a letter saying it was the most profitable lesson he had ever learned.

We can all make better use of our time by following a few simple suggestions. Countless hours are squandered by people who have no scheduled plan for their day's work. Depending on your job and position, scheduling may not be completely under your control; however, even then there are many things you can do to organize your time that will enable you to accomplish much more and raise your work production.

Scheduling applies to all areas of life. The homemaker who runs to the grocery store five times a day wastes time. She would be further ahead and have much more time by simply scheduling her day's activities. Trips to the school, grocery store, department store, gas station, ball game, hospital, etc., could be accomplished in, possibly, one-third of the time with proper scheduling. Such organization can also save gas, as well as wear and tear on the car and your nerves.

Setting Priorities

Considering six to eight hours of sleep per night, everyone has sixteen to eighteen hours of manageable time each day, right? Wrong! Most of us waste a great majority of our time. At work and at home, we could accomplish much more by setting priorities. Some things can wait, while others must be done right away. Certainly, completing a major project on time is more important than filing a few papers, and a visit to a sick friend is more important than mowing the yard. The danger, however, is to fall into the trap of procrastination and never do the less important things. Get it all done, but the urgent should be at the top of the list.

A Typical Morning in the Office

At 8 A.M. Jim is asked to get some forms out of the safety file. On the way to get them, the phone rings and he's told that he is late on the sales report to his boss. As he hangs up, he gets another call to come down to

the computer room. He lays down his files and heads over to the computer room to discuss the problem. On the way over, he meets a friend and stops for a cup of coffee. By the time he finishes the coffee and gets up to leave, he has forgotten what he came for. He returns to his office. The phone rings and he gets into a conversation about tomorrow's plans. He looks at the clock and it's five minutes until twelve, so he leaves for lunch. His morning has been extremely busy—running here and there, answering phones, gathering safety files, and visiting over a cup of coffee—but so far he hasn't accomplished a thing. Does this sound familiar?

Telephone Rules That Save Time and Money

Much valuable time is wasted on the telephone. The following simple guidelines will save you time—and sometimes money.

First, if you are on the receiving end of a call that is going on too long, simply say, "Thanks for giving me a ring, but I need to go—do—see about—check—fix—take my medicine—take a nap—cook—or whatever." Of course, be sure that what you are saying is true and

don't tell a fib. Obviously, you must properly evaluate whom you are talking with, the friendship involved, and the understanding each party has of the other. I don't know how many times I have heard people say, "I just can't get off the phone," thus wasting precious time.

Next, if you are making a business call, state the purpose of your call clearly, slowly, and concisely. Don't repeat yourself.

Then, listen carefully to the information you receive and repeat it back if it involves dates, addresses, phone numbers, or names. I don't know how many hours I have wasted because someone has failed to accurately write down the proper information.

Finally, when you make a call, don't wear out your welcome. After all, your friends may have work to do, too.

Visitors and Salesmen

Depending, of course, on whether a visit is at home or the office and whether it is personal or business-related, there are many ways you can reduce wasted time. I am not talking about visits with close friends and social visits that we really appreciate. I am talking about the visitors or salesmen who wear out their welcome, maybe not intentionally, but through a course of habit.

First, if your time is limited—say so; and let them know that they will have to be brief. A good way to communicate that time has run out is to politely stand up behind your desk, make a short comment, and thank them for their visit, while taking a step or two toward the door. It will work almost every time, and no one is offended.

Again, social visits need special treatment, but even these can be handled in hospitable ways so that you can stay on your time schedule.

The Paper Shuffle

"I can't find my desk! Oh! There it is, under all those papers!"

Many executives and office workers waste half their time shuffling papers—looking for lost memos, documents, pencils, and everything imaginable. Their desks look like a tornado just blew through. Taking a few minutes to organize your desk, room, office, or home is a must.

Write It Down

You may think you don't need to make notes because you have a good memory. Well, with one telephone call to your wife, husband, or boss, I can shoot that excuse down. There are a number of ways to make notes. Keep notepads in convenient locations. Keep a day planner or memo pad in your kitchen, den, office, purse, or pocket to record dates to remember and important things to do.

My son, John, has a little, black notepad in which he writes down everything he needs to do and check on. Every time we meet, he flips through his pad and says, "Dad, how about this? Have you done that?" A simple procedure, but it works. He calls it his "brain" and says he would be lost without it.

The calendar on the wall is a good place to write down important future dates and events. This will save you the embarrassment of going to someone's home for a dinner date on the wrong evening. It may also save you from showing up for a job interview a week after the job is filled.

Organization—Who Needs It?

The arrangement of an office and home is so important. The dishwasher does not belong in the bedroom, and the refrigerator does not belong in the den. Likewise, your office tools should be organized and in their right place. Your desk, filing cabinets, storage bins, etc. are the necessary tools of your trade. But they can become thieves of your time if not organized and placed where they can be used effectively.

File It

A good filing system is a must in every home and, of course, in every business. Your home filing system should include files for recipes, keepsakes, warranties, instruction manuals, phone numbers, addresses, news clippings, ideas, and articles on various subjects of interest—just to name a few.

The sooner in life you begin your filing system, the better. The organized material will be valuable in years to come and will save you countless hours of looking for things you might have lost. If you don't already have one, invest in a good filing cabinet and start your filing system today.

File every piece of paper immediately. You should only touch a piece of paper once. Handle it and file it. If you put it in a pile to be filed, you will constantly be going through that pile to see if what you are looking for is there. File it immediately.

Countless hours are lost looking for birth certificates, immunization records, deeds, insurance policies, sales contracts, promissory notes, and mortgages. Let's say you bought your home and made the last payment five years ago. Now you have sold the house. The lawyer calls and says that, in checking the title, he finds a mortgage still on the property at the courthouse.

"I paid that note off five years ago," you say.

"Maybe you did, but there is still a mortgage against the home for $75,000, and we can't close the deal."

You panic and call the bank that financed the home for you. They tell you the records show they mailed you the mortgage note five years ago, marked "Paid in Full." It was your responsibility to go down to the courthouse and get the mortgage taken off the records. Maybe you thought that since it was paid, there was no need to keep it, and you threw it into "file 13." Well, too bad. Your lawyer will have to go to court and get the judge to officially cancel the note in order to clear up the mess. In some states, you will even have to post a bond. This is costly. What a mess! You may even lose your sale. All because you have no filing system.

I've gone through this myself because I or an employee misfiled a paid-off mortgage note and never had it cancelled. The same day I reviewed this chapter, I spent about half the day looking for a mortgage note that was paid off approximately five years ago. I had a real estate closing at 4:00 P.M. and received the news that the mortgage was still on the courthouse record. The bank couldn't find it and could find no record of ever having mailed it to our office. Not our fault, right? Well, not completely. We should have followed up shortly after the payoff, reminding them that we needed the paid-mortgage note. This would have saved a lot of time and lawyers fees.

Yesterday-Today-Tomorrow
Eternity

When tomorrow comes, it will be now, and now will be yesterday. Yesterday was now before tomorrow became now. Now was once tomorrow and yesterday was once now.

The only time you have is right now, but it will become yesterday before you can blink your eye. We live each moment between two vast periods, yesterday and tomorrow, but we cannot live the present moment in either of the two, even though they are only a microsecond away.

THE
MYSTERY OF TIME

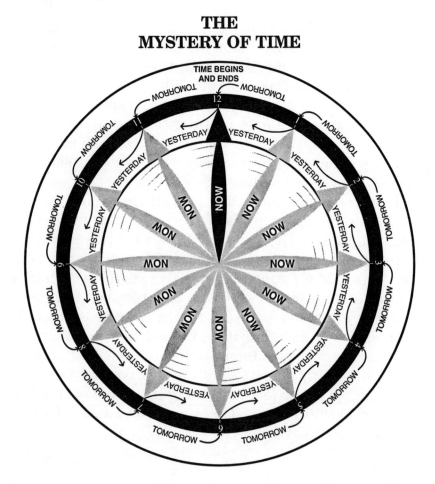

Try to visualize time as a big clock with only one hand, representing the now. Tomorrow constantly turns into now only to become yesterday. Finally, the circle is completed, at which time the clock stops, and time is no more. There are no more tomorrows, and yesterday is frozen into one eternal now, the forever present. Just maybe in this way we can envision the vast eternity we are traveling towards.

Time and life are inseparable. Time has witnessed all of history unfolding and permits it to march on. God outlined time's mission when he created the moon and sun. He put a canopy of space over our heads and sprinkled it with billions of glittering stars. Time never slumbers or stops to rest. Time will continue its mission until the day God stops its march and announces, "Time shall be no more." We all have yet one final appointment with time.

Just as man is destined to die once, and after that to face judgement (Hebrews 9:27).

In the beginning, O Lord, you laid the foundations of the earth, and the heavens are the work of your hands. They will perish, but you remain; they will all wear out like a garment. You will roll them up like a robe; like a garment they will be changed. But you remain the same, and your years will never end (Hebrews 1:10-12).

In the meantime, pay careful attention to your money tree's branch of Time. It can be your friend or your enemy, depending on how you use it. Time has helpful hands full of good things, but will not wait nor can it be recalled.

---

*As if you could kill time without
injuring eternity.*
— Henry David Thoreau

CHAPTER TEN

Thankfulness

*Enter his gates with thanksgiving and his courts
with praise; give thanks to him and
praise his name.*
— Psalms 100:4

Where Are the Nine?

Jesus was the greatest storyteller of all time. He was able to take the simplest happenings in life and from them draw unforgettable lessons.

On one occasion, ten men who were dying of the dreaded disease, leprosy, approached Jesus and cried out, "Have pity on us!" Jesus simply told them to go show themselves to the priest; and as they turned to go, all were instantly healed (Luke 17:14).

One of the ten lepers was a Samaritan. The Samaritans were half-breeds—part Jew/part pagan. Great animosity and hatred existed between the Jews and the Samaritans.

In this story, we find a poor, despised Samaritan, who had the disease of leprosy, living with nine Jews who had the same disease—a rather strange group. There is something about disaster and pain that bring people of like problems together, no matter what the past may be. In this setting, a remarkable thing occurs.

This lone Samaritan returned to Jesus, fell down at his feet, and gave him thanks. Jesus then asked, "Were there not ten cleansed? Where are the nine?" Ouch! Only this despised, cast-away Samaritan returned to say "thank you."

Too many times, this question can be asked today. "Where are the nine?" When was the last time we said thank-you to the postman, waitress, grocery clerk, cashier, neighbor, or fellow employee? "Oh," we say, "but that's what they get paid for." But is that really relevant? Maybe they have a sick child, a mother in the hospital, a recent death in the family, a tragic divorce, or some other heavy burden. What they need at that moment is a smile, a thank-you, a pat on the back, or a warm hello. *"A word aptly spoken is like apples of gold in settings of silver"* (Proverbs 25:11).

A person's whole day can change for the better when someone notices their need and speaks a word of kindness. Even the grouchiest person cannot resist a little kindness. Our thankfulness or lack of it gives insight into our character and is a picture of our heart.

A Special Day

One cold, dreary, January morning, a woman braved the freezing rain to come to my office. She asked the receptionist if she could speak to me. I invited her in.

I wondered what she wanted, as over the years I had been conditioned to such visits. Complaints, requests for loans, family problems, and dozens of other situations had been presented to me at one time or another.

This woman stood before me, approximately fifty years old, dripping wet from the cold rain. I thought that what she had on her mind must be mighty urgent for her to get out on such a cold, rainy day.

I was humbled by what she told me. Now, brace yourself.

She said: "Mr. Howard, I work in one of your stores and have been an employee of yours for many years. I just wanted to tell you how much I enjoy working for you. I count it a privilege. My family and I are grateful that you have provided me this job. I just wanted to say thank you."

I was almost speechless; I was not prepared for her gratitude. After these many years, I can still see her standing there on that cold, wet, January day—an ordinary woman offering a simple "thank you."

I must confess that the memory brought a tear to my eye as I penned this story.

Page Two

On that same day, one of our executives made a purchase in one of our stores across town. As he was checking out, he spoke to the cashier. She began complaining about how miserable the day was, how she didn't like her new job (this was her first day), that the pay was lousy, and that this was a miserable company to work for. This was her first job and I had recommended her to the store management.

The company executive reported this rudeness to the manager, and she was dismissed the next day. No company can afford to have that kind of personality as a representative of its business.

Comparing her to the woman who offered the "thank you," the young girl probably possessed the greater potential of the two because of her youth. However, unless her outlook has radically changed, she probably is still on the bottom of the heap somewhere, wondering why everything always goes wrong in her life. Hopefully, she has learned that such a negative disposition leads to disaster. The difference between the two women was in the heart.

Appreciation

Our perception makes a world of difference in our attitudes.

After completing grade school, during the depression years, we were bused about seventeen miles to a school in the city to complete our education. To us country kids, this was a big step up.

I soon noticed that the "city" kids had pretty, store-bought lunch boxes, while we had only paper sacks or syrup buckets. I also noticed that they had sandwiches made with store-bought white bread and real, store-bought sliced meat (baloney), while we country kids had homemade biscuits, thick cuts of smokehouse country ham, stuffed sausage, and fresh, hen-house eggs.

We thought we were really moving up when we traded our country food for those store-bought goodies. My, my, how that ol' country cooking has improved with the years, and somehow that store-bought stuff just doesn't taste like it used to. In fact, now I catch myself driving miles just to find some good ol' country cooking.

You just don't miss the water until the well runs dry!

Important Words

Listed here are some key phrases that we all need to learn and practice:

The five most important words—"I am proud of you."

The four most important words—"What is your opinion?"

The three most important words—"If you please."

The two most important words—"Thank you."

The least important word—"I."

— Source Unknown

The First Thanksgiving

The first Thanksgiving proclamation was made by Governor Bradford three years after the Pilgrims settled at Plymouth:

To all ye Pilgrims:

In as much as the great Father has given us this year an abundant harvest of Indian corn, wheat, peas, beans, squashes, and garden vegetables, and has made the forests to abound with game and the sea with fish and clams, and inasmuch as he has protected us from the ravages of the savages, has spared us from pestilence and disease, has granted us freedom to worship God according to the dictates of our own conscience; so I, your magistrate, do proclaim that all ye Pilgrims, with your wives and ye little ones, do gather at ye meeting house, on ye hill, between the hours of 9 and 12 in the day time, on Thursday, November ye 29th, of the year of our Lord one thousand six hundred and twenty-three, and the third year since ye Pilgrims landed on ye Pilgrim Rock, there to listen to ye pastor and render thanksgiving to ye Almighty God for all his blessings.

— William Bradford, Ye Governor of Ye Colony.

Not Everybody Does

An old farmer sat down in a fancy city restaurant and ordered breakfast. The breakfast was served and he bowed his head to offer thanks. The other folks sitting nearby snickered at the old man and asked, "Old Timer, does everyone say their prayers where you come from?"

"Nope," the old farmer replied, "the pigs don't."

A genuine cultivation of your thankfulness branch will bring rich rewards.

---

*If you have been living in Grumble Thicket,
how about moving up to Thanksgiving Avenue?*

CHAPTER ELEVEN

Work

I went past the field of the sluggard, past the vineyard of the man who lacks judgment; thorns had come up everywhere, and the ground was covered with weeds, and the stone wall was in ruins. I applied my heart to what I observed and learned a lesson from what I saw: A little sleep, a little slumber, a little folding of the hands to rest—and poverty will come on you like a bandit and scarcity like an armed man.
— King Solomon, Proverbs 24:30-34

The Peril of Idleness

In the year 109, the Roman legions that were left behind to rule a defeated Spain built an aqueduct in Segovia. This aqueduct carried water to the Segovians for 1,800 years.

Around the turn of the twentieth century, the Spaniards decided that the aqueduct should be preserved for posterity. They built new, modern pipelines and stopped the flow of water that for years had gushed through the aqueduct.

Shortly thereafter, the aqueduct began to fall apart! The blazing hot sun dried the mortar and made it crumble, and soon it fell into ruins. What many centuries of service could not destroy, crumbled when it was left idle.

"He Who Always Looketh for Easy Work Will Go to Bed Tired"

"Opportunity knocked on my door today. He was dressed in work clothes, so I sent him away."

Have you ever noticed that the harder a person works, the luckier he becomes? Success is made of hard work, persistence, faith, and vision. Work may be the "old-fashioned way," but it works.

Call the Doctor

If your money tree is sickly, stunted, or not producing, you may just need to call the money-tree doctor. Dr. Cure is an expert in treating sick money trees.

Some of the symptoms Dr. Cure looks for are: sleepy eyes, loss of energy, bedsores, obesity, and heavy debts.

He has found several diseases that accompany these symptoms: TV-itis, Sportmania, Tablehernia, Pepsiulcer, Analysisparalysis, and Procrastitosis.

Warning! If Dr. Cure's instructions are carefully followed, radical improvement can be expected. However, the medicine may bring a certain amount of discomfort for the first six months.

Habit forming? Yes.

Long-term effects: Improved health, restful sleep, increased energy, and less dependence on others.

Unless these diseases are detected and treated, they are sure to kill your money tree. Dr. Cure has a sure remedy. In fact, he hasn't lost a case yet. The cure is a bit painful, but it doesn't cost a penny, and you don't need a prescription. The cure is called *"work."*

A Job Well Done

"Lazy hands make a man poor, but diligent hands bring wealth" (Proverbs 10:4). Well said, King Solomon. A little digging, fertilizing, pruning, and watering will work wonders for a sick money tree.

"God blessed them and said, 'Fill the earth and subdue it'" (Genesis 1:28). Work is honorable. It gives dignity and hope to mankind, it builds character and is fulfilling. The rewards are numerous and are not only measured in dollars, but also in contentment, self-respect, and achievement.

The quality of my work represents the pride I have in myself. My name is stamped on each piece of work I turn out. My signature says one of two things: "half-finished, poor quality, ragged edges" or "top quality, first-class, genuine 24-karat." A job well done brings self-respect. We should all do our work in such a way that when finished, we can walk away with our heads held high. We do a disservice to our company, family, and ourselves when we do sloppy, half-hearted work. We cheat others; and even more, we cheat ourselves. Always autograph your work with excellence.

Contentment

Sometimes we excuse ourselves and say, "But I don't *like* my job." Don't worry; someone else will have it before long! Have you ever noticed that the other person's job always looks easier than your own? Funny how hard-working folks have such "good luck."

Work gives us the greatest pleasure when we feel we are accomplishing something worthwhile. As the old saying goes, "We get out of it what we put into it." A recent survey showed that 90 percent of Americans are not satisfied with where they live. Since approximately 25 percent of the American population moves each year, within a four-year period there is a complete turnover. Sounds like the proverbial dog chasing his tail. No job is perfect, but your attitude can make a tremendous difference.

The Big Picture

One problem is that the modern factory assembly line isolates the worker from the big picture. All of us want to feel that we are an important part of the whole. When we fail to see the whole, it becomes easy to lose interest in our job. Management is as much at fault as labor. Management often fails to educate employees concerning the vital part each one plays in his job. As a worker, I need to see that shiny new car moving off the assembly line as my product and be proud. The end result is hard to see if all I have done is screw in the headlights or oil the robot track. I must see the big picture in order to feel a part of the team.

Sometimes, a spacecraft launching will fail because of one small screw, a loose bolt, or a disconnected pipe. Hundreds of millions of dollars are wasted because of seemingly insignificant things. The worker probably did not realize the importance of his single job.

"Let 'er Fly"

A man was given a blunt ax and hired to chop wood. The pay was very good, but after a few hours the man quit. The reason? "I have to be able to see the chips fly," he said.

We all want to see the "chips fly." We need to know that we are making a contribution to our family, company, and society. When we enlarge our vision, we are able to see the big picture, and our jobs have more meaning and are more fulfilling.

The Importance of the Work Ethic

"Be sure you know the condition of your flocks, give careful attention to your herds; for riches do not endure forever" (Proverbs 27:23-24).

The work ethic is at the root of the American success story. Our pioneer forefathers braved a hostile environment, broke new ground and planted farms, blazed trails through the wilderness, built cities and roads, laid the railroads from East to West and North to South. How did they do it? By faith and hard work. What was their reward? The most prosperous nation in all history. What will keep it that way? Faith and hard work. What will cause us to lose it? Lack of faith and hard work. It's that simple.

Faith and hard work are indispensable to success. Without them, our factories and goods will become inferior and our products too costly to compete in world markets. In this regard, America is slipping badly. We must turn our heads and focus our eyes on these old, traditional, tried-and-proven, work-ethic principles. Our schools, businesses, factories, churches, and families must combine efforts to teach these principles. All Americans need a good healthy dose of work-ethic principles.

As the walls of Communism crumble and the Third World countries begin to use more products produced by other nations, competition will escalate in the world market. We must be ready for this challenge. Sadly, we are already running behind.

East Germany is a showcase for the fact that the work ethic makes a decided difference. The workers of East Germany suddenly find themselves competing with the traditional work ethics of the West Germans. The industrious and hard-working West Germans, once a defeated people, have rebuilt their land, which was destroyed in World War II, and have emerged as the most powerful economic force in Europe. West Germany has become a leader in world exports and quality goods. Contrast this with East Germany, which lost its competitive spirit, its quality consciousness, and its work ethic after forty-five years of Communist domination. Their factories are in ruin, the atmosphere and rivers polluted, their stores are practically empty, and their goods are inferior. Their only salvation lies in the hands of their West German brothers and God Almighty.

The super powers of tomorrow will be those with economic muscle: pocketbook power will ultimately win over "gunpowder." The stage is already being set for the new economic super powers, namely Japan and Germany. The work ethic, or lack of it, will be a deciding factor. You cannot fool the marketplace for long with inferior and over-priced products.

The American Workforce

If you asked me to rate today's employees compared to those fifty years ago when I first entered the retail business, I would respond as follows:

First, I would say that there are thousands upon thousands of dedicated, well-trained employees in every field, who are far above average and who rate as high as, or even above, any in years gone by. I would also have to say, based on my observation and experience, that on the average, the American workforce has deteriorated very noticeably. My conclusions are based on the decline of: productivity, commitment, honesty, moral values, discipline, promptness, positive attitude, appreciation, and the three R's (reading, 'riting, and 'rithmatic).

But there is a positive note in all of this. While a continuation of this downhill trend will bring economic and moral bankruptcy to our nation, it also presents a tremendous challenge to all of us—especially to the leaders in business, schools, government, churches, and the American society in general.

If we are able to accomplish a revival of the American Spirit of sacrifice, dedication, hard work, and moral values, then America will truly become a trusted world leader and will be able to provide a solution for the many problems that face every nation. Should we fail, our military strength will not provide a solution but will only make enemies. No nation, regardless of its size, will be able to control or lead the world at the point of a gun. Moral and economic leadership are necessary.

Wanted! Gold Diggers

"There's gold in them thar' hills!" But you've got to dig it out. Ultimately, the public decides what my job is worth or even if I have a job. I must produce a product or service that is a benefit to mankind and society. Not only must I produce a product that is a benefit, but it must also be at the right price. When I or my company fail to pass these two criteria, watch out—trouble lies ahead. When these criteria are not met, my job is not secure and the company's survival is in jeopardy.

Success does not come by accident. It is the reward for providing what society needs—at a price they are willing to pay. It's that simple.

Perfect People

Work is a people business, and people can be problems. Some won't work! One employee came into my office one day and said she was looking for the perfect job. I told her I knew exactly how to find one.

"How?" she asked.

"Find one without people."

As long as there are people, there will be problems; but these problems provide opportunities to serve, challenges to overcome, and goals to reach. After all, who is going to buy our services or products? You guessed it—people. And get this—"people with problems." The work of the world does not wait to be done by perfect people.

Bruce Barton once said: "If you expect perfection from people, your whole life is a series of disappointments, grumblings and complaints. If, on the contrary, you pitch your expectations low, taking folks as the inefficient creatures which they are, you are frequently surprised by having them perform better than you had hoped."

A Word of Caution

I have said a lot about hard work and dedication, but I do not want to leave the impression that earning money is to become your dominant goal in life The biblical warning is certainly applicable here: *"For the love of money is a root of all kinds of evil"* (1 Timothy 6:10). Do not let it become such a priority that it becomes a god.

I do not want to leave the impression that one needs to be a workaholic. The biblical principle of one day of rest out of seven is not without good reason. Some of the greatest tragedies of life have occurred because a parent, husband, or wife spent night and day working. They spent little time with the family and, ultimately, lost their most precious possession. Laziness is not good, but work to the neglect of the family is tragic.

Try This On

Here are twelve things that I believe make a good worker:

1. A positive attitude
2. Honesty
3. Dependability
4. Good communication skills
5. The ability to listen
6. Good health
7. The ability to manage time efficiently
8. Enthusiasm and cheerfulness
9. Patience
10. Decision-making skills
11. A courteous and polite demeanor
12. The ability to motivate others

When you master these twelve things, your work branch will be weighted down with "George Washingtons."

You cannot push anyone up the ladder
unless he is willing to climb himself.
— Andrew Carnegie

CHAPTER TWELVE

Leadership

When a country is rebellious, it has many rulers,
but a man of understanding and
knowledge maintains order.
— Proverbs 28:2

Why is it that people will follow one leader almost anywhere, while another leader can't get people to follow him even to a candy store? The answer lies in the quality of the leader. Leadership begins with preparation and then is built on a solid foundation of trust and respect.

Line Up Here
The tombstone read as follows: "Dear friend, today as you pass by, as you are now, so once was I. As I am now so shall you be. Prepare today and follow me."

The following postscript was scribbled beneath the engraved words: "To follow you I'm not content, until I know which way you went."

Knowing Your Way Around
A good leader must know where he is going. While some may follow a leader through blind allegiance, they are nevertheless convinced their leader knows where he is going.

Jesus said it like this, *"If a blind man leads a blind man, both will fall into a pit"* (Matthew 15:14). Blind leaders are dangerous because they act as if they know the way and innocent followers are led to a tragic end.

Fairness and Concern

Good leaders must possess a sense of fairness. Everyone likes to be treated with respect. To be unfair and rude or to use others for ones own personal glory is wrong. Leaders must care for their troops. The concern for their welfare is of utmost importance and will have a telling effect.

In the Persian Gulf war, there was quite a contrast between the coalition forces and the army of Saddam Hussein. The Iraqi commanders cared little for their soldiers' safety and provided little protection or training. In many cases, their troops did not have even the basic necessities. Compare this to the way the allied commanders provided every conceivable protection and all necessary supplies to make sure their troops were well cared for. No American soldier ever doubted that his leaders were concerned about their welfare. As a result, they were ready to risk their lives by the thousands. Now contrast this with the Iraqis who deserted their ranks and surrendered by the thousands. Their morale was gone, and they had no heart to fight.

Character—Commitment—Loyalty

A good leader must believe he has a good cause. It is difficult to get people to give their money, time, and effort to a cause that has little purpose or value. The greater the cause, the more important the leader, and the more devoted his followers will be. A cause may be more worthy than its leader, but it will not rise to its potential without good leadership.

A good leader is seen as well as heard from. General Robert E. Lee is considered by many historians, as well as those of his day, to be the greatest general of the civil war, even though he was on the losing side.

General Winnfield Scott, the hero of the Mexican-American war, said this of General Lee: "If the President of the United States would tell me that a great battle were to be fought for the liberty of the slaves of this country and ask me for my judgment as to the ability of a commander, I would say with my dying breath, 'Let it be Robert E. Lee.'"

Well, Lee got his chance on April 18, 1861, just four days after the fall of Fort Sumter. Lee was summoned to Blair House by President Lincoln and was asked to be the field commander of the entire Union Army. Lee said he wanted to think about it and returned to his home across the Potomac. That night he walked around in his garden and pondered the decision he had to make. Virginia, his beloved state, had seceded from the Union the day before. He had said that he would sacrifice everything but his honor to preserve the Union. He also personally opposed slavery. By midnight, Saturday the 20th, he had made his decision: "I cannot draw my sword against my native state." He resigned from the United States Army. He just could not bring himself to fight against his beloved state. Loyalty and honor won out, and President Lincoln lost his first choice for commander of the Union Army. You cannot help but admire such a person, whether friend or foe.

As commander of the Southern army, his troops loved him dearly. Why? Because he was a soldier's soldier. By fighting by their sides, he endeared himself to them.

Lee's sterling character and demeanor not only won the hearts of his soldiers, but also the respect of the Union generals.

Follow the Leader

It is told that President Coolidge once invited some Vermont friends to dine with him at the White House. His friends were worried about their table manners. They decided to do everything the President did—that certainly would be correct, they reasoned. The dinner went along well until the coffee was served. President Coolidge poured his into his saucer. The guests followed suit. The President then added sugar and cream; the visitors did likewise. Then, the President leaned over and gave his to the cat.

No company can rise above its leadership. On the top of every business sits someone in charge, making decisions and setting policy. Even though several people may have input into decisions and policy making, someone still has to say, "Let's do it." As the old saying goes, "The buck stops here."

Like a lid on a tea kettle, leadership sits on top of the stove, whether it just lets off steam' or allows ideas to flow.

Characteristics of a Good Leader

When you stop to analyze what it takes to be a good leader, you may be amazed that these principles also apply to the growth of your money tree and its health.

Successful leaders do not badger, belittle, threaten, or constantly prod their associates. Skillful leaders operate on a different level; they use praise and appreciation to motivate. This does far more to correct an employee problem than criticism—and the positive effects will last much longer. An effective leader can even motivate the average person to do above-average work.

A good leader does not isolate himself from his employees. They cannot follow one they never see. Listening and observing your people at work gives new insight into their abilities as well as potential problems.

Many employee problems start as molehills and develop into mountains because of lack of attention from the top level.

The good leader is willing to accept suggestions and put them into practice. It does wonders for employee morale. It shows them that the boss is willing to listen and take advice. A leader may be knowledgeable, but he is not infallible and does not know everything. After all, an employee should know more about a machine that he has worked with eight hours a day for a year than the boss, who never spent one hour with it.

A good leader will recognize this and will listen to the suggestions of the lowest employee on the totem pole. In many areas, that "lowest employee" knows more than the company president. A good leader will thank the employee for his suggestion and not look bored while listening. The old brush-off is easily detected. A suggestion box hung in the store or shop is a great idea. The more employees are allowed to participate by sharing ideas to help make the company grow, the harder they will work to accomplish that growth.

Leadership Qualities

The qualities of a good leader are numerous. I have gathered a list of forty-three attributes of a good leader. Learn and implement these qualities, and you will be on your way toward being the kind of leader who can make his area of responsibility flourish.

A good leader:
1. Has a positive attitude
2. Is a decision maker
3. Can motivate people
4. Practices honesty and truthfulness
5. Expresses thankfulness and appreciation
6. Radiates enthusiasm
7. Knows his field of work

8. Exercises patience
9. Communicates well
10. Knows how to handle criticism
11. Sets goals
12. Works hard
13. Treats others with kindness and consideration
14. Plays as a team man
15. Is committed to excellence
16. Shares authority
17. Suggests rather than commands
18. Accepts blame
19. Is a good loser
20. Mixes well with fellow employees
21. Does not criticize anyone in front of others
22. Keeps his promises
23. Maintains an open door
24. Provides encouragement
25. Is a self-starter
26. Is prompt
27. Manages time well
28. Is orderly
29. Is precise
30. Does not watch the clock
31. Has vision
32. Generates creative ideas
33. Is a person of action
34. Brings things to completion
35. Is a people person
36. Serves others
37. Is loyal
38. Uses good judgment
39. Is a person of wisdom
40. Respects others/himself
41. Presents himself well
42. Gets results
43. Knows the facts

The Buck Stops Here

A good leader must always be willing to accept responsibility for failure, as well as for success. The old excuse that George is to blame will not work for long. For good or ill, a leader must be ready to accept the responsibility.

Please Help Me

I still chuckle when I remember the story about the man who asked the passerby if he had seen any soldiers. "Yes, they went that-a way."

The man responded, "Thanks, I'm their leader."

Diligently develop the qualities of a good leader, and your leadership branch will keep your money bank running over.

Doing something will solve more problems than saying "Something must be done."

CHAPTER THIRTEEN

Praise and Motivation

A man finds joy in giving an apt reply—
and how good is a timely word!
— Proverbs 15:23

We have all heard or read true stories in which an injured person is trapped under a burning vehicle. A rescuer picks up the vehicle all by himself and saves the helpless passenger with superhuman strength.

Don't ever underestimate the power of motivation. Wars have been won by its power and lost by the lack of it. The mind possesses tremendous power when properly motivated. We all know how contests and prizes can fire us up. Our children are perfect examples of what can be accomplished with a little positive motivation.

He Made Me Do It

John had been on a wild boar hunt and was returning to the camp after shooting all his ammunition. Suddenly, a wild boar with tusks six inches long charged from the brush, slashing at John's heels. Luckily, just a few feet away was a large tree with a limb about thirty feet above the ground.

John sized up the situation in a split second: The hog was about to slash him wide open, and the tree was too big to reach around and climb. Even if John could climb the tree, the wild hog would surely attack before John could get out of reach. His only option was to jump up to the limb that was thirty feet above his head. Jump he did, and with all his might—but he missed the limb. However, he was fortunate and caught it on the way back down! Motivation makes a lot of difference!

"I Ain't Gonna Sign It!"

One company was having trouble signing up a lone dissenter in its insurance program. The company needed his participation in order to put the policy in effect, but he had been bad mouthing the insurance plan among the other employees for weeks and was adamant that he would never sign up.

The boss finally had enough and called "Jim" into his office for a face-to-face meeting. Mr. Smith may not have used the best method, but he got the job done. He leaned back in his chair and calmly said, "Jim, you are a good employee, and I am sure you are a sensible man, weighing the facts carefully before making a decision. We have an excellent new insurance program, much better than the old policy, with very little extra cost. All our employees have signed up, except you. I would like to convince you to change your mind and sign this enrollment card. If you choose not to sign, we will have no hard feelings toward you. You have every right to make up your own mind and say no. However, the payroll department already has your final check cut and signed. You have my permission to pick it up on the way out."

Jim swallowed a couple of times, hastily leaned over the desk, and signed the enrollment card.

The next day when all his fellow workers heard about Jim's change of mind, they were astonished. "Jim," they asked, "what caused you to change your mind on the insurance program?"

"Well," Jim responded, "frankly, no one had ever explained the program and its benefits to me quite like Mr. Smith did yesterday." A little motivation properly applied works miracles.

While emergencies and impending disaster will motivate a person, this spur-of-the-moment impetus often does not last past the emergency. In fact, the same person who was motivated to lift the car by himself finds the task impossible under normal circumstances, no matter how hard he tries.

People are better motivated by praise. Sincere praise for loyalty, good work, honesty, promptness, and enthusiasm are all excellent ways to "pat" someone on the back.

"My Favorite Store"

A woman who had just moved to a small town from a big city complained to a neighbor about the poor service in the local drugstore.

The next time she visited the drugstore, the druggist greeted her with a big smile, told her how good it was to see her again, and said he would be happy to do anything he could to help her family get settled. He then filled her order promptly.

Later, the woman reported the miraculous change to her neighbor. "I suppose you told the druggist how poor I said the service was."

"Well, not exactly. I hope you don't mind, but I told him that you were amazed that he had built up such a fine business and that you thought it was one of the finest run drugstores you had ever seen."

A Moment of Praise is Worth More Than a Month of Criticism

Praise will go a thousand times farther than criticism. You will be surprised how much change will come over a friend, family member, employee, or even an enemy when you give praise. Praise motivates people to excel in whatever they do. Their work habits will improve and their outlook on their job, and even their life, will change for the better. Nine times out of ten, a gentle "pat on the back" accomplishes more than a swift kick on the bottom.

All of us want to know that we are appreciated and needed. People want to know that what they do contributes to the success of the company or project. Employees, as well as family members, need to feel wanted and important. Failing to recognize this principle causes much dissension and many problems.

Don't wait until something goes wrong before you take note of a person. If you will notice what people do, show concern about their hopes and accomplishments, and ask questions, this will communicate that you have a personal interest in their welfare and success. Constant harping about the bad things while ignoring the good things, will not inspire and motivate anyone. As important as good pay is, many will work harder,

even at lower wages, if they feel the boss cares about them personally and is interested in their problems as well as their successes.

A daily "laying on hands" (a sincere pat on the back), together with sincere praise and helpful suggestions, will bring amazing results. Praise and appreciation breed enthusiasm. Enthusiasm, coupled with less-than-perfect knowledge, will carry a person farther than intellect alone. Enthusiasm is like a cold: it's catching.

Most of us find it easier to criticize than to offer praise. Yet, almost without exception, a person will work harder and accomplish more under the spirit of praise than under the spirit of criticism. Even when criticism is needed, it should be done in a constructive, rather than destructive, way.

Criticism may make people work harder for the moment because they have to; but with praise, they will continue to work harder and accomplish more because they want to.

Encouragement is oxygen to the soul.

"You're Doing Fine"

A machine has been developed to measure fatigue. In the test, the doctors were astonished to discover that by saying "You are doing fine," they could make the energy curve soar. These simple words of encouragement were like a shot of adrenalin. Faultfinding had the opposite effect.

This branch on your money tree, when properly nourished, will keep money in your checking account.

Any ornery old mule can kick down a barn,
but it takes a carpenter to build one.

CHAPTER FOURTEEN

Criticism

Better a dry crust with peace and quiet
than a house full of feasting, with strife.
— Proverbs 17:1

While praise and appreciation are powerful tools in dealing with people, there is a definite and legitimate place for criticism.

Confronting another person concerning a wrong done is one of the more difficult aspects of communication. It is especially difficult to do in a manner that brings positive results. Confrontation can be beneficial, but it must be handled in the right way. First of all, our own attitude must be right. We must not feel smug about the opportunity to point out the wrong of another person. To the contrary, we should be sorry that the confrontation must take place. At the same time we must realize that a well-handled confrontation can actually help the person who made the mistake to grow.

Sometimes it is easier to simply fire the employee or take away the job that was mishandled. But this solution may cause you to lose an overall good employee; and often, with a little help, they can actually gain the skills needed to do better next time. Or we might reason: "Well, this is the first time Junior has set fire to the house. He has been a good boy for two hours, so I'll not say anything to him right now. I'll wait and see if he burns it down on the next try." But handling a small problem promptly will keep it from growing into one that is not so easily remedied.

If criticism is necessary, it must be thoughtfully and swiftly dispensed in order to achieve positive results. I would suggest the following thirteen principles.

1. Make sure you know the facts—undeserved criticism is a morale killer.

2. Don't criticize in front of others.

3. Explain that the purpose of your criticism is to help.

4. Never criticize while in a fit of anger—cool off first.

5. Start with praise for some good thing the person has done. Be genuine; there is something good in the worst of us. We tend to forget the ninety-nine good things a person may have done and allow the immediate

incident to get completely out of focus. Of course, this does not justify the wrong, but with the exception of Junior, there is usually justification to show appreciation. It will be easier for the person to accept criticism if they know you have their best interest at heart.

6. Let them know up front that you are disappointed with their behavior and that you expect better things out of them. In using this approach, you appeal to their "better side." This is a powerful incentive. We all have a "built-in" desire to please those around us, especially those in authority.

7. Let them know that such behavior is unacceptable. Point out how it affects their own welfare and the welfare of others.

8. Pause and give time for a response. Be a good listener. Hear their side of the story. Listening is an art that tells a person you are interested in what he has to say.

9. Provide positive ways for them to correct their failure. By doing this, you highlight their problem, but you also suggest solutions.

10. During your dialogue, try to find some common ground or mutual interest. Use this common ground to make the person feel that you are on their side.

11. Threats of additional action should be tempered to "fit the crime." Is this the first or the tenth visit? Do not "overkill."

12. Remember, there is no place for petty grudges in healthy working relationships.

13. Sign off on a positive note, with positive expectations.

It is important that you cover all these major points, even though you may get a confession and a promise to do better early in the conversation. All of these points help reinforce their commitment to reform. If you will be thorough, you may save another conference and also keep the house from being burned down.

This branch should not be left unattended, or it will produce rotten fruit and contaminate the whole tree.

The three hardest words: "I am wrong."
The next three hardest words: "You are right."

CHAPTER FIFTEEN

Anger

A gentle answer turns away wrath,
but a harsh word stirs up anger.
— Proverbs 15:1

No doubt about it, anger gets us into a lot of trouble, and our pride will keep us there. Anger is like a pot full of boiling water: If you allow it to overheat, it will boil over on you. Anger is as dangerous as a match in a gunpowder factory. One spark and it will blow up the whole plant.

Many foolish, cutting, and senseless words have been spoken in fits of anger. Relationships are destroyed and character is ruined because of uncontrolled anger. The tongue is a mighty weapon, and we must choose our thoughts and words wisely. *"My dear brothers, take note of this: Everyone should be quick to listen, slow to speak and slow to become angry"* (James 1:19).

A person is as big as the things that make him angry. You can tell a lot about a person by how easily he becomes angry, how long he stays angry, and what he gets angry about. The Bible tells of a man named Jonah who showed what kind of heart he had by what made him angry. A vine that provided shade for him died, and he told God, "I am angry enough to die." Jonah's folly was that he was more concerned about his vine than about the thousands of people living in the nearby city of Ninevah.

Anger: Both Good and Bad

All anger, however, is not bad. Anger has both destructive and constructive power. What sane person does not become angry when they see another human being abused and mistreated. Appropriate anger can move us to seek solutions. The way we handle our anger is the key. But even "righteous anger" must be held under control. You must find constructive ways through which you can bring about change and positive results.

Jesus, himself, displayed anger. When he saw the priest and leaders of his day deliberately robbing, cheating, and misusing their authority and position, he strongly rebuked them.

First Cousins

Anger, pride and greed are first cousins. Each one feeds off the other. When one gets in trouble, all three are usually there.

Your money tree is in trouble if you let these three villians take charge and rule your life. Greed will cause you to bypass the patience branch. Anger will cause you to lose your reasoning power. And pride will justify it all. *"Pride goes before destruction, a haughty spirit before a fall."* King Solomon (Proverbs 16:18).

Simple But Powerful Tools
For Dealing With Anger and Disputes

Never respond to rudeness with rudeness.
"Reckless words pierce like a sword, but the tongue of the wise brings healing" (Proverbs 12:18).

Guard your speech.
"He who guards his lips guards his soul, but he who speaks rashly will come to ruin" (Proverbs 13:3).

Practice self-control.
> *"A fool gives full vent to his anger, but a wise man keeps himself under control"* (Proverbs 29:11).

Agree where possible. A response that says "You just might be right" does wonders.
> *"Starting a quarrel is like breaching a dam; so drop the matter before a dispute breaks out"* (Proverbs 17:14).

Keep your "cool."
> *"A hot-tempered man stirs up dissension, but a patient man calms a quarrel"* (Proverbs 15:18).

Back away and give it time.
> *"A fool shows his annoyance at once, but a prudent man overlooks an insult"* (Proverbs 12:16).

Anger is a universal problem and seemingly has always been so. The Bible is full of advice and warnings concerning anger.

This one final thought from the Bible: *"Do not be quickly provoked in your spirit, for anger resides in the lap of fools"* (Ecclesiastes 7:9).

A money tree cannot long stand if a careless mouth shoots off the branches. Hold your fire.

Alcohol and gasoline do not mix.
Neither do money and anger.

CHAPTER SIXTEEN

Listening

He who answers before listening—
that is his folly and his shame.
— Proverbs 18:13

The Value of Silence

My friend, speak only once, but listen twice.
This I would have you know is sound advice.
For God hath given you and all your peers
A single mouth, old friend, but a pair of ears.
— Author Unknown

A close friend of mine, a bank president, told me the following story:

He had called a special board meeting to discuss a sizeable investment in a project that would also include some outside financing through other banks.

The major stockholder of the bank was a spinster lady, and, to say the least, she was an unusual person. On the day of the meeting, she arrived with "Charles," her chauffeur, who was also her handyman. She requested that Charles be allowed to sit in on the board meeting. Well, how do you say no to your major stockholder? So Charles took his place, along with the directors and visiting bankers. Charles sat there, dressed in his work clothes, listening to the discussion. The board members, not aware of the situation, were quite puzzled and kept glancing out of the corner of their eyes at Charles, wondering who in the world this character was.

After a lot of discussion, the proposition was brought to a vote. Charles had sat there through all the proceedings, not saying a word and taking in all the discussion as if he were profoundly interested in the outcome. In reality, he hardly knew the difference between a checking account and a certificate of deposit.

As the vote proceeded around the table, it came time for the major stockholder to vote. At this point, she leaned toward Charles and asked him what he thought about the deal. The eyes of every banker and director were focused on Charles. Slowly, Charles leaned back in his chair, took a long, slow draw on his big cigar and then slowly exhaled, letting the smoke circle around his head. He took another long draw, exhaled slowly and looked as if he were in deep thought. Finally, he leaned forward and without speaking a word, gave a slow, but definite, approving nod.

The motion was carried and the meeting adjourned. The bankers and directors left, scratching their heads and wondering who this man was. Was this Charles an intelligent man? You bet he was. Intelligent enough to keep his mouth shut! How many of us would have opened our mouths and shown our ignorance? We all learn more from listening than talking.

It takes courage to speak up, but there are times that it takes more courage to be quiet and listen. Trouble is, when you talk too much, you usually say things you haven't thought of yet.

Have you ever been awakened in the night by one barking dog, then before long every dog in the neighborhood was barking? Well, people are somewhat like that—a lot of barking, but only one "dog" knows what he's barking at.

He Heard the Tick

One day a farmer was helping in the seasonal chore of stocking an icehouse when he lost his watch. Loudly bewailing his misfortune, he set about with his lantern and rake, hunting for it in the sawdust on the icehouse floor. His companions joined him in the search, but their clamorous seeking failed to turn up the timepiece.

When the men went to lunch, a small boy slipped into the icehouse and found it. Asked by the astonished owner how he had accomplished the feat, the youngster explained, "Well, sir, I just lay down in the sawdust and kept very still, and soon I heard the watch ticking." Few of us realize the value of listening.

Foot-in-Mouth Disease

A guest at a concert leaned over to the man beside him and commented on the woman singing. "What a terrible voice! Do you know who she is?"

"Yes," was the answer. "She's my wife!"

"Oh, I beg your pardon. Of course it isn't her voice, really. It's the stuff she has to sing. I wonder who wrote that awful song?"

"I did," he replied.

Enough said. Time to listen.

Listening is a "must" branch on your money tree. Listen. You might just overhear this branch talking to your banker telling him to transfer funds from your checking account to your savings account.

Even a fool is thought wise if he keeps silent,
and discerning if he holds his tongue.
— Proverbs 17:28

CHAPTER SEVENTEEN

Decisions

Multitudes, multitudes in the valley of decision!
— Joel 3:14

Joe was hired to work in the potato field to sort out the good potatoes from the bad. His friend came by one evening to visit and noticed that Joe had lost a lot of weight and looked terribly worried. "Joe," said his friend, "this potato job must be about the hardest work a person could do—bending over all day in the hot sun, working long hours, and sorting those potatoes. You're working too hard."

"Oh no," said Joe. "It's not the bending over or the long hours that's getting me down, it's having to make all those decisions."

Decisions can make us or break us—financially, physically, and mentally. Many a business or family has gone "bust" because of a bad decision or no decision at all.

Adolf Hitler made a fatal mistake in World War II by making a wrong decision. He had already conquered Western Europe and had England on her knees. But

instead of invading England and finishing the task, he
decided to invade Russia. The rest is history . . .

No Decision is a Decision

In addition to making wrong decisions, the inability
to make a decision will absolutely paralyze a person or a
company. Even if you are on the right "track," you'll get
run over if you just sit there. Decision-making is a
must. A company executive once said, "You won't get
fired for making a decision, even if it's wrong, but you
will get fired if you make no decision."

Learning to Make Decisions

Everyone seems to be waiting for something.
Psychiatrist William Marston asked 3,000 people,
"What have you to live for?" Ninety-four percent were
only enduring the moment—waiting to take that long-
dreamed-of trip, waiting for children to grow up, just
waiting.

The big problem is that time for waiting eventually
runs out and you are still standing in line.

Once you make a decision, it is imperative that you
follow through and complete the task. Those who spend
too much time deciding where to begin will find it is too
late to start. Five things will help cure the habit of
procrastination in your decision making.

1. Make a list of things you have a tendency to put
   off.
2. Set specific dates as goals to have projects
   completed.
3. At the end of each day, review your work to see if
   you accomplished what you said you would.
4. Make sure you obtain the necessary know-how. We
   tend to put off things we do not know how to do or
   understand.

5. Tell others what you are going to do. Then your word will be at stake.

We all have a tendency to ignore the big problems, rather than face them and make a decision. Indecision is like trying to jump a stream in two hops. In making a decision, just give it your best and then . . . jump.

The trick of being a good decision-maker is to avoid unwarranted delays on one hand, without making too quick, snap judgments on the other. Following are some guidelines to use in making major decisions:

- Take sufficient time to understand the problem.
- Make a list of choices.
- Make a list of the positive results of each choice.
- Make a list of the negative results of each choice.
- Bounce your thoughts off associates and friends (two heads are better than one).
- Consider your options.
- Ask yourself: What will the short-term effect be? The long-term effect?
- Develop a backup plan just in case the decision doesn't work.
- Incorporate flexibility into the plan.
- Pray for wisdom.
- Once a decision is made, do not be too quick to reverse it or too slow to change it, if it is not working.

Changes are difficult in many cases, and some foot dragging usually occurs if many people are involved or affected. But if you will take the time to educate people as to the reasons for a change, it will be better accepted.

Decide now to hold this branch on your money tree in high esteem. It will produce a lot of fruit during the dry season and enable you to buy extra Certificates of Deposit.

Think like a man of action;
act like a man of thought.
— Henri Bergson

CHAPTER EIGHTEEN

Patience

A patient man has great understanding,
but a quick-tempered man displays folly.
— Proverbs 14:29

The sign on the preacher's office read, "Lord, give me patience, and give it to me right now."

We live in the instant generation: a hurry-up, worry-up, warm-up, get-up, bust-up world. We've got instant coffee, instant tea, instant cereal, instant soup, and instant TV dinners. Such conveniences have conditioned us to expect instant answers to all our problems, instant cures for our headaches, and instant wealth. We're in a hurry to get nowhere so we can hurry back to somewhere. We are impatient at the red light, at the checkout counter—at everything we do. We honk our horns at the drop of a hat. One driver got out of his car after being honked at for a couple of minutes and said, "Mister, I'll honk your horn for you, if you'll try to get my car started." Patience is something you admire greatly in the driver behind you, but not in the one ahead of you.

The old proverb that says "Rome wasn't built in a day" is still true. Trees do not grow tall overnight; babies do not become adults in six months; and to expect a harvest before the rain and the hot sunshine and a storm or two is unnatural.

Long-Winded Preachers

We are even impatient at church. We are in a hurry to leave at the last "Amen" in order to beat our neighbors to the cafeteria. One Sunday, a stranger entered the church as the sermon was about to end. After a couple of minutes, he began to fidget. Leaning over to the old white-headed man at his side he whispered, "How long has he been preaching?"

"Thirty or forty years, I think," the old man answered.

"I'll stay then," decided the stranger, "he must be nearly through."

I Want It Now

How difficult it is to be patient. The young teenager wishes he was twenty-one, while his mother wishes she was sixteen again. Young-married couples want a new car, a new house, and new furniture, despite the fact that Mom and Dad worked many years before they were able to buy such things. How frenzied we get when our dreams are not fulfilled at once. How easy it becomes for us to be impatient with our friends and associates. How many times has our own impatience brought to naught great undertakings?

One Thousand Failures

It is said that Thomas Edison, the great inventor, failed one thousand times before finally inventing the light bulb. His associates were ready to quit long before the eventual success and questioned his wisdom in wasting so much time. His response was that he had actually made a significant discovery. He now knew one thousand ways it would not work! His persistence finally paid off. And now the world is full of light because of one man's patience.

My Bean Pole

When I was a little boy, my mom and dad would give me a handful of seed as they planted the spring garden so that I could plant my own little row of beans. I would carefully make a little furrow, drop my seed into it, and

gently cover it up with some nice, loose soil. Then I would sprinkle a little water over the soil and look forward to the day my beans would sprout. Every day I would go out and look at my little row of beans, hoping to find them bursting out of the ground. However, by the third or fourth day, my patience would reach its limit. I would dig my fingers into the soil to see how the beans were doing, and, of course, in the process, I destroyed the little sprouts and the roots that were beginning to take hold. In about a week to ten days, I would look over at Mama and Papa's rows, and the earth would be cracking open, and little heads would be popping out and dancing in the sunlight. Few, if any, of my seeds ever made it. I would destroy them in my impatience. I soon let the grass and weeds take over the few that did survive, as they required more patience and care than I was willing to give. I never recall getting a single bean from any of my rows.

True Success

The important things in life cannot be bought at the supermarket. Success, wealth, character, relationships, happiness, contentment, and good habits are not in the instant-food department. All must be nurtured, cultivated, worked at, weeded, and given lots of TLC. Then, with time and patience, we will develop the positive characteristics and successful life that we desire. *"He is like a tree planted by streams of water, which yields its fruit in season and whose leaf does not wither. Whatever he does prospers"* (Psalms 1:3).

By a patient, fruitful life we provide branches of shade for the weary and limbs loaded with good fruits for the hungry. The key ingredient is patience. Oh yes, you read stories of the instant wealth that a few obtain, but don't count on it happening to you. "Money does grow on trees," but it takes hard work and patience.

Thrown Into a Think Tank

One of America's greatest industrial inventors was a man who was patient and believed in what he was doing. For many years, he was considered a failure and was deeply in debt. In 1838, he made a remarkable discovery, but he was penniless and was forced into bankruptcy. He intentionally insulted a judge so that he would be thrown into jail and have more time to concentrate on his goals. What a think tank! While there, he perfected his new invention. In the end, he paid off all his creditors and made a fortune for those who had believed in him. Today his name is a household word. No doubt, you have ridden thousands of miles with his name under you and have seen his name floating high in the sky. His name was Charles Goodyear. He discovered the method of vulcanizing rubber. His patience and persistence finally paid off.

Seed Corn

At the end of the harvest season, my papa would select the finest and biggest ears of corn. My brothers and I would have the job of shucking them. Papa would then take the corn and store it safely away until springtime. After the fields were plowed and rowed the following year, we would plant the corn that we had carefully saved. Papa would make some scarecrows and place them all around the field to protect the freshly-planted seed corn.

This was all very exciting to us boys. However, in the trees along the fence rows, a bunch of black crows would sit—watching and waiting. Just as soon as we would finish planting and turn our backs, they would dart in, scratch up the seed corn, and have a feast. They somehow seemed to know exactly when planting time arrived. The crows didn't know it, but for every grain of corn they dug up and ate, they destroyed a stalk that would have produced a sackful. "What shortsightedness!" We would have explained this to the crows, if only we could have communicated with them.

Their concern was for the present. So it is with us. Our own personal crows always seem to show up at the right time—planting time. In our impatience, our crows eat up the seed corn to satisfy our instant desires and demands. And in the long run, we are the losers.

Lessons From the Barrel

By the way, many of the crows were also losers. Papa did have a way of communicating with them. Many crows paid for that one grain of corn, that instant dinner, by having their heads blown off with Papa's long-barrel shotgun. What was an instant dinner became instant death.

A healthy branch of patience must grow on your money tree. It will produce extra dividends just when you need them most.

There is no great achievement that is not the result of patient working and waiting.
— Josiah Holland

CHAPTER NINETEEN

Experience

He who riseth late must trot all day.

When an employer considers who to hire, experience is always at the top of the list.

"Know-how," in one sense, is like money in the bank. Most jobs require training; however, the individual who already has know-how and experience will move up to the top of the class.

How Do You Get Experience?

We have all heard the question, "Which came first, the chicken or the egg?" The question of how to gain experience is a similar one: It's hard to get a job without experience, and you can't get experience if you can't get a job.

Trying to get experience on the job, without the necessary education, can sometimes be dangerous and costly and surely comes harder and slower. I can offer no better advise than this: use every possible opportunity to learn—whether in a classroom or talking to and learning from qualified people. Learn all you can, while you can, about everything you can.

You cannot be an expert in every field of endeavor, and at some point in life you must focus on a chosen field; however, you never know when your miscellaneous knowledge will prove useful. Life always brings unexpected turns, and sometimes these turns lead to "happy trails." The preparation and knowledge you acquire along the way will pay big dividends when the road turns.

Do-Re-Mi-Fa-So-La-Ti-Do

In mid-summer, after all the cotton had been hoed and the cornfield had been plowed for the final time, a two-week singing school would begin. To us kids it was a great time and a big relief from working in the fields in the hot July sun. It was a chance to be with all the other kids, as well as the adults of the community. Papa and Mama made sure that we learned our "do-re-mi" scale. This was our vacation.

Little did I know what those singing-school days would mean to me later in life. At the time, it was just a good place to be—instead of out in the cotton and corn fields. Thirty-five years after those summer singing schools, what I had learned led me into the publishing business. In 1970, I edited and published my first church hymnal which has now sold over two million copies around the world. Just recently, I published a new edition due to the demand for an updated version.

I have received letters from many parts of the world, thanking me for publishing my song book. A friend of mine visited Poland recently and was invited into a Polish family's home. There on the piano was my book, *Songs of the Church*. It made my friend feel right at home. The Polish family could hardly believe he was a friend of the editor.

I never dreamed, while sitting in those hot classrooms, how valuable those singing-school summers would prove to be. Many years have gone by and millions of dollars in sales have resulted from those days of preparation.

Right Verse, Wrong Song

Experience is only valuable if it is in the right areas. When I was a small boy, we had community "hog-calling contests." The winner of the contest was perceived to be quite a person of talent and accomplishment. It was an honor to be named the best and most experienced hog caller in the community. I can still see my Dad, with a big smile on his face, as he exercised his hog-calling skills. However, I would not recommend pursuing a hog-calling career in today's market place, no matter how much expertise you may have in the art. There are a lot of ads in the classified section of the newspaper, but I don't recall seeing any for hog calling, lately.

Rabbit Chasing

Many people have a lot of experience—but not always in the right areas. Experience is what we get when we were expecting something else. Much time is lost in what I call chasing rabbits, "running to and fro throughout the earth," chasing things that amount to nothing. These rabbits never are caught.

Just down the street from where we lived was a family who had a dog named Shep. Every time a car turned the bend, Ol' Shep would charge out, hair bristling, and chase the car down the road. You would have thought he was going to chew the tires off the rims. This went on day after day.

I can just imagine the following scenario: Ol' Shep comes home late in the evening, with his tongue hanging out and hardly able to walk.

"Well, Shep, how did the day go?"

"Mighty good, mighty good."

"What have you been doing all day?"

"Chasing cars."

"How many did you catch?"

"Actually, none, but I got real close to one or two."

"Shep, it's time to go out and round up the cows and bring them in for the night . . . You can't go? Why not? Oh. You're too tired from chasing cars."

This goes on year after year until finally Shep is told to get out and find himself a good-paying job. No more of this car-chasing business as he hasn't caught one yet. (It would be interesting to know what Shep would do if he ever did catch a car.)

Well, Shep goes down to Fido's Meat Market, talks to Fido himself, and applies for a job in the dog food department. "Shep," asks Fido, "what kind of experience do you have in selling dog food?"

"Really, none," Shep responds. "I've only had experience in chasing cars."

Fido: "How long have you been chasing cars?"

Shep: "Some ten years now."

Fido: "Ever caught one?"

Shep: "Nope, but I've gotten mighty close a few times."

Fido: "I'm sorry, but we need a good dog who has some experience in selling dog food."

The next day, Shep goes down to Spot's Hog Farm. Spot is looking for a good hand, but no luck—same story. The next day, off to Barker's Sheep Farm, then on to Bulldog's Cattle Ranch, all to no avail. Shep finally winds up at Car Chaser's, Inc. and notices a "Help Wanted" sign. This is right down Shep's alley. The owner interviews Shep, and finds that Shep has all the necessary qualifications and experience. The company just lost a fine dog employee and needs a replacement. "How long did the other dog work?" Shep asked.

"Oh, about ten years. He was a fine car chaser," answered the owner.

"Did he retire?"

"Yes, permanently. He caught his first car yesterday."

Many people are just like Shep. They go through life chasing rabbits and cars, never gaining any real skills.

They apply for that high-paying job down at the factory or department store, and on their application under "Previous Employment" they list ten different jobs for the past ten years. Really, they have been "chasing rabbits." Stamped across the application is a reject and this note: "No opening for rabbit chasers."

Let me give you a tip. Personnel managers look very carefully at your employment record and how often you have changed jobs. Of course, many times there are good reasons for the change of jobs, such as the type of work, a business closing, and the necessity of having to move. However, when a person constantly changes jobs for no good reason, his name goes to the bottom of the application list. It is too expensive to train new workers only to have them quit and move on. A consistent pattern of changing jobs every few months will kill your chances of being seriously considered for employment in most companies. When you give references, your former employers will not recommend you. If you don't give references, then the company to which you are applying will sense something is wrong. You are in a catch-22 situation.

The Zap Treatment

There is hope, however, for car chasers. A friend of mine has a collar that he puts around his dog's neck. When Ol' Shep starts to chase cars, he simply pushes a button on the remote control and transmits a zap to Ol' Shep.

A neighbor of mine had a dog named "Suzy" that was an avid car chaser. In fact, she caught one once, and now, she's a three-legged car chaser. To prevent her from losing another leg, my friend put the collar on Suzy. After several days of zapping, Suzy decided to retire from the car-chasing business.

Some wives would like to fit their husbands with a zap collar. A few zaps might work when the wives need the husband to run some errands!

Experience, learning, hard work, and sweat are musts, if you are to be ready to take advantage of that new job opening or promotion. There are no shortcuts to knowledge and experience in the marketplace.

Climbing the Ladder

When you can say with confidence that you have done the job well, then you are on your way to advancement and a better paycheck.

Take advantage of every learning and training opportunity available. There may just be a better way to save time, money, or materials, and a way to make a better product. You may be the only one who can make it happen!

On your money tree, be sure you have a good, healthy branch of experience. It will put a lot of extra money in your money market fund. But remember, no car chasers!

The cost of living: Good judgment comes from experience and is sometimes paid for out of bad judgment.

SECTION III
BRINGING IT ALL TOGETHER

CHAPTER TWENTY

Sue and Jim—
The Big Trap

Cast but a glance at riches, and they are gone,
for they will surely sprout wings and
fly off to the sky like an eagle.
— Proverbs 23:5

Why are so many in such a financial mess? One contributing factor is the good ol' American tradition of "keeping up with the Joneses." (This works fine until the Joneses refinance.)

The "buy now and pay later" syndrome literally drowns many people. Actually, it's really the "pay forever" plan. Just like a whirlpool in a river, it will suck you under. The person who thought up that easy-payment slogan deserves a trophy. Easy for who? At 21 percent interest and higher, it's just about as easy as flying to the moon and back without a spaceship.

Financial Pressure

Lack of money-management skills is a fundamental cause of many family breakups. One survey showed that 50 percent of all divorced couples list finances as a major factor in their divorce. Financial pressure is a contributing factor in many suicides, heart attacks, mental breakdowns, and crimes—all because money-management skills are lacking.

In this section, I will give guidelines and principles that, if followed, will help you avoid the pitfalls of financial pressure and keep your finances on sound footing.

Happy Days Are Here Again

Let's take a look at an imaginary couple. We'll name them Sue and Jim. Sue and Jim represent far too many American families. I have witnessed their predicament many times.

Sue and Jim are newly married. Most of their lives, Mom and Dad have fed them, clothed them, and put shelter over their head. The parents even paid for their college education. Now, they are starting a new life. The wedding bells are still ringing, and they think they can conquer the world—no matter that Alexander the Great and Napoleon failed!

Almost before the wedding congratulations have died down, Sue and Jim's mailbox is filled with beautiful bargains and a myriad of offers. Every bank in town invites them to open an account, offering many exciting advantages. Letters from VISA, Mastercard, American Express, Discover, Exxon, Hertz, Avis, jewelry stores, and the finest department stores in town arrive daily. Jim and Sue are on everyone's list. All sorts of incentives are offered—no interest, special discounts, free gifts—just to get them to sign up.

Acquiring credit cards is so easy! A man was recently arrested who had a warehouse full of merchandise he had ordered using credit cards. The total cost? $200,000. He said that he didn't even know what to do with all his purchases, but he kept ordering them because it was so "easy." Surveys have shown that purchases increase approximately 30 percent per shopping trip when credit cards are used. I might add, so does the debt (the law of cause and effect).

The Life of Riley

Jim: "Why Sue, I had no idea so many people knew us. Judging from all these credit card offers, we must be pretty important! We've got it made and haven't even gotten started yet." So Jim and Sue sign up, and a few days later the credit cards come rolling in. In fact, Jim's wallet won't hold them all, so Sue goes down to "Kneeman's Sock-em Store" and picks him out a fine new eelskin wallet.

Cashier: "Mrs. Smith, we want you to know how pleased we are to have you shop with us. You have such good taste! May I have your charge card to finish your purchase?"

Sue: "I think I'll just pay cash today."

Cashier: "Oh no! You need to establish your credit, and now's a good time."

Sue: "Hhmm . . . that sounds easy!"

Cashier: "Oh yes!"

Sue: "Well, just hold the wallet. I'll be back in a minute." Sue rushes back to the dress department where she saw that beautiful spring outfit that would look so good on her and that would really please Jim. She adds this to her purchase and leaves happy.

Cashier: "Come back soon, Mrs. Smith! You have such lovely taste. We're here to help you any time."

Well, the stage has been set. Let's follow Sue and Jim down life's road as the weeks and months pass.

Jim and Sue's income is $1500 per month. What you are about to see can and does happen regardless of a person's income.

Jim and Sue's Monthly Expenditures

Jim and Sue have no budget to follow, and they don't record their checks in their checkbook. (This is a sure sign of impending disaster. It is imperative that you record every check you write, that you balance your checkbook daily, and that you reconcile your checkbook every month.)

I wanted to know how Jim and Sue spent their money, so I had a couple of elves follow them around for a month, and this is what I found:

Club dues	$ 25
Apartment rent	450
Car payment	250
Utilities	100
Food	250

Clothing (credit plan payment)	125
Recreation	50
Vacation (credit plan payment)	100
Boat (credit plan payment)	100
Insurance	75
Gas and oil	100
Small medical bills	50
God	1
Grand total	$1,676
Monthly income	$1,500
Overspent	(176)

Up until this point, Sue and Jim are happy. They're living the life of Riley, but Riley is about to move out. They have overspent $176 for the month. But since they have no budget, they don't know it and "what you don't know won't hurt you," right?

The American dream is about to turn into the American nightmare!

Murphy's Law begins to come into play: "Anything that can go wrong *will* go wrong."

A Serious Illness
Jim has an appendicitis attack and is admitted to the hospital. They think: "No problem, we have insurance." But even then, they have to pay $500 out-of-pocket.

A Newsletter From Their Favorite Banker
Last year Jim cosigned a note at the bank for an old buddy. (Jim has forgotten about it.) Now his "old buddy" has quit making his payments and won't return the banker's calls (a definite sign that he *can't* pay). The banker calls and says, "Jim, I'm sorry, but you'll have to pay your buddy's five hundred dollar note." (Everybody is sorry except Jim's buddy, who is now his enemy.)

I got a call from a banker one time, too. I had cosigned a note to help one of my friends get started in business. My friend had been telling him that he would pay off his loan as soon as he got "all his ducks in a row." The banker, after hearing the duck routine several times, called me at my office and said, "Alton, your friend is way behind on his payments, and he's been lining up his ducks for quite some time. I'm sorry to have to tell you, but you'll have to line up 100,000 George Washingtons in a row."

Accident!

Jim arrived at the office two hours late, and the boss asked him what was going on.

"As I was coming in this morning, some idiot ran into me from behind and the stupid rascal didn't have liability insurance."

"That's terrible, Jim," replied the boss.

"Oh well, my insurance will take care of it."

The next day Jim calls the insurance company: "What do you mean I don't have any insurance?"

The insurance representative replies, "We didn't receive your premium."

That night at home: "Sue," asked Jim, "why didn't you pay our insurance premium?"

"You said we needed to save money and that we didn't have the cash. After all, you said, you were a careful driver."

"How was I to know that some nut without insurance would run into me from behind? It's going to cost a thousand dollars to fix the car."

"What was the fellow's name who ran into you?"

"Some guy by the name of Murphy."

Murphy's Law is slowly, but surely, taking over.

Rent Increase

The landlord called today, and Sue and Jim's rent is going up $50 per month.

Legal News!

Today, Jim got a notice from a lawyer by certified mail that said he was being sued for $5,000 for running over a neighbor's dog. Their baby's pet! Registered, too!

"There's no way they're going to get away with that," Jim says. "That dog wasn't worth twenty-five dollars! I'll get me a lawyer and beat that deal." Sure enough, he was right. The judge said Jim only had to pay $25.

Jim: "Well, for once, justice won out! It pays to get the best lawyer. I wonder what he'll charge?"

The Friendly Banker Again

Today, Jim got another call from the bank saying that the "no-way-to-lose" deal he got involved in last year just lost. Jim is asked to come down and pay off the $5,000 he borrowed, since the security is no longer good. It must be paid at once as the bank examiners are coming next week. $5,000 due! Jim can't pay, so he goes down to the local finance company and borrows the $5,000 at 25 percent interest to pay off the first loan which was at 10 percent interest, and he mortgages everything but the kitchen sink. (He's definitely making progress—backwards.)

Company Bankruptcy

Jim comes home, has a good night's sleep, and dreams that all his problems are solved. (Not exactly, the sun hasn't come up yet!) The next day, Jim is informed that the company where he works is filing bankruptcy. Now, his payments get even further behind. After many phone calls and threats from bill collectors, he reads one of those nice ads about consolidating all your bills into one "easy payment" plan (about as easy as swimming the English Channel). He goes down to yet another finance company and puts a second mortgage on everything at 33 percent interest. He comes home and sleeps like a "baby" (wakes up screaming every hour), thinking that everything is solved. (Again, not exactly. The first payment hasn't come due yet.) He later finds out that the monthly payments barely cover the interest, and he'll be paying for the next fifteen years.

Surprise, Surprise, Surprise

Jim has been out all day looking for a new job, and Sue finally runs him down at a friend's house. "Jim, you're wanted on the phone. Your wife is calling."

Jim: "Yes, Sue? What?? Twenty-five hundred dollars!! The lawyer's bill for that dog case I won last month?! Why that sorry, no-good rascal. I knew he was a crook from the beginning."

Good News, But Wrong Timing

Jim comes home after a hard day of looking for a job and Sue says, "Guess what, honey! I have good news tonight."

Jim: "What?" (Remember Murphy's Law.)

Sue: "We're going to have a baby!"

Jim: "Just wait until I get my hands on that Murphy guy!"

They have no insurance, so they'll have to pay the hospital up front.

More Good News

Jim comes home with really good news. Just in time, he got that new job—not only a new job, but one that pays twice the salary he made before. "What luck!" Jim says, "Well, old Murphy is not so bad after all. You just have to hang in there." ("Hang" in there is right!)

What Jim and Sue don't know is that another of Murphy's laws is about to kick in. It says, "Our 'necessity bag' miraculously expands to include what was before in our 'want bag.'" Put into layman's terms: "My 'needs' will always rise to the occasion and a little beyond."

Here We Go Again

With a new baby, the house is too small, so Sue and Jim rent a bigger house at a higher cost. Now they need a bigger car, bigger vacation, and more clothing. After all, they make twice as much money now. Everything is lovely for a few months, but soon the same old unexpected things begin to happen all over again. The difference this time is that Jim and Sue owe twice as much. It now costs them about two and a half times more to live than it did before because of higher interest costs and their higher standard of living.

Jim's Bright Idea

Jim: "Well, Sue, no problem! I'll add up our assets and see where we stand. Wow! We're millionaires! Look at all these time-saving devices and appliances. (Yes, but they haven't the time to use them.) TVs in every room, boat and trailer (haven't used them, but they sure look impressive in the yard), riding lawn mower, vacation home on 'Lake Easy.' Look at the list of all this furniture, our insurance cash value, our investments and club membership, and all these tools. In fact, I'm really surprised. We have more assets than I ever dreamed!" (He's right, he's been living in a dream world. But he's about to be awakened.)

"Sue, we'll just sell everything, pay off all our debts, and put the balance in the bank." What Jim doesn't know yet, but will soon find out, is another law that I'll add to Murphy's. It says, "When you buy something, everybody wants one; but when you want to sell it, everybody has one." The bottom line is: what you pay for something is not what you can get when you sell it.

So they dispose of everything, at about 35 cents on the dollar, and have to move in with Mom and Dad. They still owe half of their debts and are worse off than ever.

A New Beginning

The tension continues to mount for Jim and Sue. The debt, the squabbles, the stress of facing bill collectors, and the constant blame finally do them in. They file bankruptcy, and their marriage crumbles. Both Jim and Sue remarry. Of course, their new partners are much "smarter" than the first ones. Because they are so smart, they know that they will have no problem keeping up with the Joneses. Being smarter, they live a little higher and faster, making up for lost time. Of course, this round will be no different than the previous one—only a different street address. It is just a matter of time before Murphy's Law takes over and poor health, wrecked emotions, and bad attitudes lead to serious problems, and another family will fall apart.

Jim and Sue never understood their problem. They never realized that the root of their problem was poor money management, combined with Murphy's inevitable Law. To beat Murphy's Law, you must know the rules and you must have a defense fund.

You may think the story of Jim and Sue sounds a bit far-fetched, but it is very real and is repeated over and over every day. The root cause is lack of money-management skills. So many people have to learn from the College of Hard Knocks. The trouble is, most people who go through the College of Hard Knocks get knocked out before they graduate.

When you find a path with no obstacles,
it probably doesn't lead anywhere.

CHAPTER TWENTY-ONE

<u>Debt—The Killer</u>

By wisdom, a house is built,
and through understanding it is established;
through knowledge its rooms are filled with
rare and beautiful treasures.
— Proverbs 24:3-4

"Hello."
"That you, Jake?"
"Yep, this is Jake."
"It don't sound like Jake."
"Well, it's Jake all right."
"Are you sure this is Jake?"
"Sure, I'm sure this is Jake."
"Well, listen, Jake, this is Harry. I need to borrow one hundred dollars."
"All right, Harry, I'll tell Jake when he gets home."

The Debtor's Prayer
"Now I lay me down to sleep,
Little money have I to keep,
If I'm found before I wake,
The rest of it, my creditors will take."

Americans have little time to worry about the end of the world because they spend most of their time worrying about the end of the month.

Does your outgo exceed your income? Does your upkeep bring about your downfall? Is there enough left over to carry over? Is your check spent before you get it? Well, welcome to the club. You have plenty of company. Most Americans spend 10 percent more than they make, no matter how big their paycheck.

A family that earns $18,000 per year spends an average of $19,800. If you were earning $100,000 per year, you'd probably spend $110,000. Even Donald Trump had trouble with his meager $450,000 per month allowance!

Debt—Good and Bad

In today's world, money is just another commodity. We may loan it, borrow it, invest it, or spend it. Money can be a blessing or a curse. Debt can also be a blessing or a curse. Money can be our master or our servant. Debt can be our master or our servant.

Debt, per se, is neither good nor bad. The trouble lies in the abuse and misuse of debt. The big question is: Why am I going into debt?

Borrowing wisely for things that will produce a good return—such as a home, needed transportation, and even an education (when viewed as an investment)—may be a wise decision. Going into debt for pleasure and for things that you have only for the moment is not very wise.

The Danger of Debt

Debt has a way of creeping up on you somewhat like the proverbial camel who at first puts only his head inside the tent. Just as the camel soon overtakes the whole tent, debt will soon take over your whole life.

The major reason people get overloaded in debt is lack of discipline. They get their "want box" too big, their life-style too high, and allow peer pressure to dictate their spending habits.

Debt is a form of bondage. *"The borrower is servant to the lender"* (Proverbs 22:7). Master "Debt" has you. Then you begin to sing the song, "If I Can Just Make It Through December." Then along comes Master "Santa Claus," and he is really a bigger "taker" than "giver." (The reason Santa is always so jolly is because he gets all the credit while you pay for all the "goodies.") Then you hope you can make it through April 15th, when Master "IRS" is waiting in the wings. With all this compiled debt, you hope you can make it to next December, when it begins all over again.

Debt Robs Us of the Anticipation of Enjoying
The Fruit of Our Labors

We live in the instant age. We can get everything on the spot, from instant pudding to instant cash. However, this instant age deprives us of the joy of anticipation. When we finally get something we have wanted for a long time, we actually enjoy it more than if we had gotten it "instantly." Most of us experience "Christmas" many times a year. The more we have, the less we are able to anticipate the really, special occasions.

Debt Is Responsible for Many Family Problems

When we get over our heads in debt, we blame each other. "It was your fault for buying all that stuff."

"No, it's your fault. You manage the money and write the checks!"

The tension grows, and "Bill" starts to look elsewhere. He takes a liking to sweet "lazy Jane" at the office. To escape it all, he takes off with her, and there goes the family. The grass always seems to be greener on the other side of the fence. (It may be because they work harder at keeping it up.)

Cash Flow

If you have a positive net worth, but are still in financial trouble, your problem may be negative cash flow. This can be a real killer. You simply have more payments and expenses than you have income. Your income cannot service your debt load. Be careful. You may end up asset-rich, but cash-flow broke.

Leverage

Many large corporations also find themselves with a cash-flow problem, and they use leverage in an effort to solve their problem.

Leverage is excessive borrowing against a company's assets in order to accomplish certain goals. Individuals sometimes try this too. Like stretching a rubber band, all is well until the stress reaches the breaking point.

As a boy, I often watched folks crank their old Model A Fords. Occasionally, the car would backfire and the crank would suddenly reverse its direction. Some people had their arms broken this way.

Leverage is like cranking the Model A. All is well when the crank is turning to the right, but one little backfire and it will break your financial arm. A fall in real estate values, a recession, high interest rates, new tax laws, and many other factors can and do burst the bubble. Read the "obituaries" in the newspaper that tell of failed companies if you doubt me.

Using leverage may be good in certain situations, but for purely speculative purposes, the debt load can backfire and blow your financial britches off.

Bankruptcy Abounds!

Have you ever heard of Chapter 7 or Chapter 13?

From riches to rags: this is the song that 750,000 Americans sang in 1990 on the way to bankruptcy court. That figure is double the amount of cases filed in the previous five years put together. The bankruptcy rate is skyrocketing with no slowdown in sight. There will be over one million bankruptcies in 1991. One out of every 130 households will file bankruptcy. When it will end is anybody's guess.

Bankruptcy is a big price to pay for lack of money management. Many think that once they declare bankruptcy, all their troubles will be over. Well, not exactly. Your bankruptcy record will haunt you for ten years. Every credit report will show your bankruptcy record, and your credit purchases will be greatly restricted. You may not be able to buy a home or obtain a loan for any purpose. Also, IRS debts will not go away with a bankruptcy declaration. The stigma of bankruptcy is hard to shake, and there are even moral implications. When you declare bankruptcy, you have, in effect, failed to live up to your word, not to mention the financial jeopardy you may place others in.

Many times, filing bankruptcy fails to solve the problem. People who file bankruptcy often repeat their mistakes and end up going bankrupt again.

Debt By Default

My son, if you have put up security for your neighbor, if you have struck hands in pledge for another, if you have been trapped by what you said,

ensnared by the words of your mouth, then do this, my son, to free yourself, since you have fallen into your neighbor's hands: Go and humble yourself; press your plea with your neighbor! Allow no sleep to your eyes, no slumber to your eyelids. Free yourself, like a gazelle from the hand of the hunter, like a bird from the snare of the fowler.
— Proverbs 6:1-5

Do not be a man who strikes hands in pledge or puts up security for debts; if you lack the means to pay, your very bed will be snatched from under you.
— Proverbs 22:26-27

These verses are quite interesting. King Solomon must have had a lot of experience along this line, and I have had a little myself. It is usually bad news.

Never cosign a note with someone unless you are prepared to pay it off in full. Why? Because the one you are signing for is already in trouble or he wouldn't need you.

When you cosign, you are the real borrower. The one you sign for may have little or nothing to pay the note off with. If they default, the bank will look to you.

If you want to help, the best thing to do is to make the person a donation, that's probably how it will turn out in the end, anyway. That way, you will still have a friend. I'm not saying you are not to help your neighbor, but you simply need to understand that you must be able to afford the cost. If not, don't do it. I have 100,000 George Washington reasons to be an expert on this subject.

12 Warning Signals

Below are listed 12 warning signals that raise a flag to let you know you are headed for financial trouble. If over one third apply, you are headed for difficulty. If half apply, you are already in trouble.

1. Using credit cards for cash advances.
2. Being dependent on the next raise, plus a little overtime (you hope), to get your bills current.
3. Borrowing from the cash value of your insurance policies.
4. Making new loans to pay off old ones.
5. Using credit to buy luxury items.
6. Paying only the smallest amount permissible on your credit cards.
7. "Maxing-out" your credit cards.
8. Applying for additional credit cards to give you more borrowing power.
9. Borrowing money from your friends.
10. Always paying your bills late.
11. Having nothing in savings.
12. Borrowing from finance companies.

You know you are in trouble when a car pulling into the driveway, a telephone ringing, or the arrival of the mail causes you to tremble.

The Credit Card Booby Trap

Buying with credit cards has become an addiction for millions of Americans; they have become "credit-aholics"—from users to abusers.

You may find yourself "borrowing from Peter to pay Paul." "Peter" being one credit card and "Paul" being another. Many have done this until all their cards come tumbling down.

The credit card business has reached a volume of almost $300 billion and is still growing. Now, that's big business. The issuers' losses, however, are tremendous. That's why they must charge such high interest rates. The good payers have to pay for the losses from those who do not pay.

A True Case From My Files

I'll call this couple "Tim and Sally." While Sally was in college, she was issued a credit card by a major credit card company. (Get 'um while they're young and innocent.) That's when it all began. Soon she had several cards. Tim and Sally got married after Sally quit college. Together they earned $1,400 per month. With the help of their credit cards, they soon ran up bills totaling $7,000. Their monthly payments left little for day-to-day living expenses. Their new, happily-married life had turned into a nightmare.

To escape their creditors, they opened a new checking account and got a new telephone number—both under a new name. They were afraid to answer the phone, and they hid from their creditors. Their life was in a turmoil, and a new baby was on the way. What a way to start married life—burdened with debts.

Fortunately, they sought counsel, cut up their credit cards, and by using the principles outlined in this book, they got back on track and have turned their life around.

Most are not so fortunate and drown in their problems. You cannot be fully secure as long as burdensome debt exists. Debt is a poison that will kill your money tree.

Six Stages in Life

It has been said that people go through six stages in their life:

> In infancy, they want fun,
> As teenagers, they want excitement,
> In their twenties, they want romance,
> In their thirties, they want admiration,
> In their forties, they want sympathy,
> And in their fifties, they want *cash*.

Don't expect your ship to come in if it is loaded with debt. It probably will sink.

CHAPTER TWENTY-TWO

Whose Is It?

Again, it will be like a man going on a journey,
who called his servants
and entrusted his property to them.
— Matthew 25:14

Lessons From the Bible

I have yet to hear of any "secret" way to become successful that ignores biblical principles. All the "secrets of the ages" can be found in the moral and ethical principles in the Bible. I know of no exception.

Many of Jesus' parables are about money and management. There are over seven hundred references to money in the Bible. Some scholars say there are as many as three thousand indirect references. God knew that money, or wealth, can be very dangerous. It can either be a means of blessing for humanity or a curse. For these reasons, God gave instructions to help us handle our money and possessions.

Whether or not you correctly handle your wealth is largely determined by your attitude toward it. Remember, "the *love* of money is a root of all kinds of evil" (1 Timothy 6:10—italics added)—not money itself. Money used or sought after for evil purposes has been the root cause of hundreds of wars, murders, and family feuds and has led to the breaking of every commandment.

The Ownership Relationship
God gives us principles of ownership and management so that we can know how to handle wealth.

Ownership is actually a relationship. Your understanding of the ownership relationship will largely determine your success or failure in money management. If we don't understand this principle, in the final analysis we will not be good stewards and we will not reach our total financial capabilities in a responsible way. Understanding this concept will change your life and your concept of wealth.

Who Owns the Store?
First, let's establish who the owner of the store is.

"The earth is the Lord's, and the fullness thereof" (Psalms 24:1—KJV). That's everything.

"For every animal of the forest is mine, and the cattle on a thousand hills" (Psalms 50:10-11).

"The silver is mine, and the gold is mine" (Haggai 2:8—KJV).

"Heaven and earth is yours [God's]" (1 Chronicles 29:11).

"You may say to yourself, 'My power and the strength of my hands have produced this wealth for me.' But remember the Lord your God, for it is he who gives you the ability to produce wealth" (Deuteronomy 8:17-18).

Try this exercise. If you own a piece of land, go down to your local courthouse and trace the title. Your lawyer did this, I'm sure, when you bought the property. It's called a title search. You'll soon discover that someone else owned it before you, and then someone before that person, and someone before that, on back to the time the Indians roamed free throughout the land. You might ask, "Where did the Indians get it?" Well, it was just there. In the final analysis, everything can be traced back to and belongs to God. We're just title holders, stewards, using and working and serving until eventually time comes to an end and he returns to claim his possessions. Therefore, we must conclude that God owns it all by reason of being the creator and the sustainer of heaven and earth and our very being.

Accountability

We are blessed with the things we hold title to. We are God's managers. But he will return and settle accounts with us later. In the story of the talents in Matthew 25:14-30, God called three of his servants to him. He was going on a journey, and before he left, he entrusted money to each of them. He left them on their own, and when he returned, he checked their bank accounts. Two of the managers did a good job and returned a very good profit. They were commended for being wise and good. The one that failed the test had buried his money because he was afraid of the responsibility. The master was displeased with his inactivity and his excuses. He cast him out, and gave what he had to the two stewards who had used their wealth in a responsible way.

It's amazing that God trusts us. He gives us the keys to the store and tells us to go and use what he has put into our hands to benefit ourselves and all of mankind. We would certainly hesitate to turn our store over to an inexperienced person or one who had been dishonest in the past. However, God puts us on our honor and tells us to manage the store and to do a good job.

Changed Attitudes

When you acknowledge that all you have really belongs to God, you will have a totally different concept of wealth and material things. With this attitude, you transfer everything over to God in your heart, and you are ready to become his manager. When you prepare your Net Worth Statement, located in the Appendix, you are asked to sign a statement acknowledging that all you have is God's. It belonged to him to start with; but with this new viewpoint, you acknowledge this fact and will have a different perspective on everything you possess. Several new attitudes result:

When you are tempted to waste something, in the back of your mind a little voice will say, "Wait a minute, is that the wise thing to do as a manager of God's store?"

It will help free you from greed and stinginess. Giving becomes a privilege, not a duty.

It will help rid you of a dependence on money for happiness. You will begin to realize that nothing is really secure in this life. Should wealth be removed from you, your life will not fall apart.

It will change your value system. Read Matthew 6:19-20. In these verses, Jesus warns us about putting trust in things; our true trust should be in God, the owner of the store.

It will help you get rid of your worry about money—or the lack of money. Needless worry about finances changes nothing.

It will give you a sense of accomplishment. By being a wise and good money manager, you can feel that you are contributing something to society. The parable in Matthew 25 concludes with the master putting the good servants in charge of more wealth, since they had handled what they had in a responsible way.

You will learn the law of sowing and reaping. (Galatians 6:7-8; Malachi 3:10; 2 Corinthians 9:6-10). Generally, we reap more than we sow (both good and bad), a principle that is evident all around us—not only in the physical realm, but also in the spiritual.

You will learn the law of sharing. 2 Corinthians 8:14-15 says, "Your plenty will supply what they need, so that in turn their plenty will supply what you need."

You will learn that a gift to others is a gift to God. Proverbs 19:17 says, "He who is kind to the poor lends to the Lord." Jesus said in Matthew 25:35-40 that when we help feed a hungry person or even offer a drink of water, we do that kindness to Jesus.

By following these thinking patterns, giving and sharing become a joy and not a burden, a privilege and not merely a duty.

The Rewards of Giving

- Giving pleases the owner (God).
- It brings help and Good News to others.
- It relieves suffering and hunger.
- It gives a purpose to wealth.
- It proves my ability to be a good manager.
- It stores up heavenly treasures that moth and rust cannot destroy. (See Matthew 6:19.)
- It enables God to entrust more to my care.
- It benefits others after I leave this earth.
- It is never wasted when given in the spirit of love (even though we may sometimes be disappointed in those who receive it).
- Through giving, we plant and receive a harvest.
- Jesus said, "It is more blessed (makes us happier) to give than to receive."

God has a bigger "giving" shovel than any of us. He wants us to be in the distribution business, not in the storage business. Our wealth should move in one side and out the other. This keeps the pipeline open and the shelves stocked for the people who need the things we are able to provide. Goods cannot flow through a clogged pipeline; neither can God's blessings.

Many times we pray for his blessings but only hold out a small cup in which to catch them. Be ready to handle what he sends you. Be a good steward—always ready to accept God's grace and ready to pass it along.

Moreover it is required in stewards,
that a man be found faithful.
— 1 Corinthians 4:2—KJV

CHAPTER TWENTY-THREE

How You Can Become
Debt Free in 24 Months

Better one handful with tranquility
than two handfuls with toil
and chasing after the wind.
— Ecclesiastes 4:6

A young married man approached the preacher, worried and very nervous. The preacher asked him what was wrong. The young man replied, "I just can't sleep, preacher. When I first got married, I worried about what my wife would do if I lost my job. Now, I worry about what I would do if *she* lost hers."

No doubt about it, debt is a killer. If a heart attack doesn't get you, worry will. If you are deeply in debt, then you were probably tempted to skip over all the preceding chapters in order to get to this one. I hope you didn't do that, because the foundation principles that have been discussed earlier are a vital part of your ability to get out of debt and stay out of debt.

If you owe a million dollars and are unemployed, I probably won't be able to help you. But if you are the typical person with an excess debt load and will follow my instructions, you can get out of debt in 24 months excluding, of course, any long-term commitments, like a house (which should be a good investment) and necessary transportation. It's not magic, and it's not complicated. It's not easy, and it does take work. But if you will really follow through, it *will* work.

Before we begin, you must make a firm commitment to get out of debt. You must want to. If you don't want to, then you won't. In order to make your plan succeed, you must discipline yourself and your family. You must make yourself go for the goal (gold). And finally, you must be willing to work, work, work!

How to Become Debt Free

Call a family pow-wow. Lay your financial cards on the table and explain your debt problem. (This may be a surprise to the kids, but they need to understand the situation and be a part of the solution.) Face the problem head on and turn it into a challenge. Set your goal: to be debt free in 24 months.

So buckle up! Tighten your belt and go for it! The plan does work, believe me, and the dividends are fantastic!

A budget is a must.

Having no budget is like having no plans for the day. You just wait to see what the day brings. One thing is sure. The circumstances of the day will be costly when the day makes your decisions for you.

A budget puts boundaries around your spending and puts you in control. A budget enables you to set priorities and lets you know if you are overspending so that you can stay on target.

A budget actually provides freedom—freedom from worry and anxieties. It gives you the good feeling of knowing where you are.

A budget is not only for the tough times. Everyone should have a budget regardless of their income level or debt situation. Following a budget doesn't have to be a sacrifice. It is simply a blueprint to insure that you spend your money as you wish.

You must first know where you stand before you can know where you are going. There are several forms in the Appendix of this book to help you do this. Copy them and use them. It is essential that you use them if you are to get out of debt.

Now turn to the Appendix and prepare the *Net Worth Statement* to determine if you are currently in a positive or negative net worth position. List all of your assets and liabilities. The difference between the two is your net worth. Your goal is to have as large a positive net worth as possible.

Next, follow the instructions in the Appendix and prepare your budget worksheets. The first worksheet, the *Budget Worksheet,* will help you determine exactly what you have available to spend and specifically how you should spend it. The *Weekly Spending Record* will help you keep up with your spending, and the *Budget to Actual Comparison* will show you how well you stayed within your budget.

If you have not been able to make timely payments to your creditors, call them and acknowledge what you owe. Let them know you intend to pay. Tell them about your plan. Tell them that you have realigned your budget and that you can pay X dollars every month until it is paid. Most will work with you if you are sincere. Remember, they can't kill you, and there is no need to promise something you can't do.

A budget is absolutely essential. You may have to set up a budget boundary line with an electric fence around it so you will get a good jolt if you try to step over the spending limit.

Generate additional income.

It is usually necessary to generate extra income in order to get out of debt. Here are a few suggestions of services that you and your family can offer on a part-time or full-time basis to earn extra income:

Answering Service   Part-time Job
Carpet Cleaning   Sewing
Child Care   Tutoring
Delivery Service   Typing
Handyman Service   Wake-up Call Service
Homemade Craft   Wedding Consultant
   and Bake Sales   Yard Work
House Cleaning

There are hundreds of things that can be done to make money. These are only a few suggestions. Don't spend this extra money on anything frivolous. Put all of it into a common pool to be applied to your debts.

You never know, but you may even be able to create a thriving new business as a result of the creative effort that you put into earning extra income. Many well-known companies had their beginnings in the basement or garage of enterprising individuals.

Spend the next couple of vacations close to home.

Think of all the "rest stops" you won't have to make! You don't have to travel a long distance to have a nice vacation. There is a lot to see and do close to home. If you simply do a little research through the Chamber of Commerce or the tourist bureau, you can have a great vacation. You'll be amazed at what goes on right around you.

Now I'm not trying to kill all the "fun," but the goal is to get out of debt in 24 months. (I wouldn't think it's too much "fun" being hounded by your creditors night and day.) Some things can wait. Anyway, a vacation that increases your debt can't really be fun, can it?

Learn to say no.

For the next 24 months, say no to every purchase that is not absolutely necessary. Do plastic surgery! Cut up all your credit cards. Surely, some things can wait for 24 months. You will be surprised how cheaply you can live.

How many long-distance calls do you really need to make? Stay at home and watch TV instead of going to the show. All the extras are nice, but if you're trying to get out of debt and want to be free from its burden, then you can do without some of these things until you are better able to afford them.

After all, how many pairs of shoes can you wear at one time? Most of us have enough in the closet to last many years, much less 24 months. How small a house or apartment can you live in? How many lights do you leave on that aren't in use? Where do you set your thermostat? You'll be surprised at what you will save on your energy bill by simply watching the thermostat. Call your local power company. They will give you some great recommendations on saving energy.

Live by the "law of affordability": If you don't absolutely need it or can't pay cash for it, then don't buy it! Most places will take "real money" if you insist.

Organize your errands.

How many trips do you make to the store every day? You make a quick trip for bread, then back for milk, uh-oh, forgot the sugar, who ate all the onions? Some people, as soon as they get home, turn around and head right back to the store. A little planning would save a lot on auto wear and tear, gasoline, and frayed nerves.

Eliminate bad habits.

By cutting out cigarettes, alcoholic beverages, even soft drinks and junk food, you can save a lot of money, as well as your health!

Be a smart shopper.

Use wisdom in your purchases. There is no room for impulse or emotional buying. Be practical in your choices. You don't have to have the newest and the best of everything. If it is absolutely necessary to buy a car, buy a used one. That new-car smell is very costly. It will disappear in a few days, anyway. If you do buy a new car, that loud bang you hear on the way home won't be a blow-out; it will be the sound of the vehicle's falling value.

Visit garage sales. You can find incredible bargains on things you really need. It has been said that one man's junk is another man's treasure. But don't buy things you don't need. (Caution: Avoid your neighbors' garage sales, as you may end up buying all your old junk back!)

Shop sales.

Shop around. Compare prices. Sooner or later, practically everything in a store will be on sale. By shopping just before or after the season, you can often save 50 percent or more.

Warning! Be careful with sales. You can go broke saving all that money. Remember, impulse buying is off limits.

Do not overbuy.

Unless the items can be used in a reasonable time, it costs money to hold excess supplies. Weigh the savings in view of the length of time it will take you to use them. They may spoil and you could spend the extra dollars on something more immediately necessary.

Put a hold on luxury gifts.

The florist has a pretty good motto: "Say it with flowers." If you must, pick some from your friend's yard. With a little planning and thoughtfulness, you can come up with an inexpensive gift that will mean even more than the one you can't afford.

Sell, sell, sell.

Go through all those unused items that are in the garage, attic, and closets and have a big garage sale. Use this money only to pay off debts. Don't go on a spending spree!

Consolidating your debt.

A consolidation loan is an option that may be helpful in certain situations. When you have a number of small debts you are unable to pay and each creditor is charging you a high interest rate, pulling these together and extending their payment over 24 months may be your only alternative.

If you want to obtain such a loan, you must first do some preparation. Make a list of all your debts along with your monthly payments. You must be completely honest and list every one. Call your creditors to be sure of the exact payoff. (Sometimes a little negotiating will get you a discount on the payoff.) Do not include your home mortgage note and any other long-term real estate debts. Review all your expenses to see what is required for basic living. Armed with this information, you can calculate how much you can afford to pay monthly for the next 24 months, and you can make a realistic budget including this payment.

Next, go to your local banker with this information and convince him of your ability to repay the loan. (I suggest you not go to a finance company. The interest rate may be 25 percent or higher). Your banker may want you to mortgage certain assets that may be freed up by paying off your debts or place a second mortgage on your home. Be completely honest with your banker and be sure you are prepared to answer all his questions. He will sense whether or not you are being honest and have all the facts. Bankers hate surprises. If you haven't been truthful, he'll find out sooner or later. A good banking relationship is a valuable asset.

See It Through

Now make a firm commitment to follow the principles and advice in this book and free yourself from the master of debt. If you follow these simple rules, you will save untold hours of worry. This plan may even save your family or your life or both!

The Benefits of This Plan Are Fantastic

- You will have more piece of mind, and we all need that.
- You will be able to start a savings plan.
- You will be able to give more.
- You may be in a position to pay off some long-term debts ahead of time, and what a saving that will be!

Celebrate!

Once you have paid off all short-term debt, invite your friends and have a party. They will be flabbergasted at what you have done. Be sure the party is paid in cash (no credit). Don't return to old habits: don't go back to the "buy now and pay later philosophy." Now you are a better manager and can do more to help others and share the Good News as a good steward of God.

The Good Old Days

The days of my youth were called the Great Depression, yet families held together, and there was little crime. The average belt size was 31 inches; now it's 38 inches. We certainly didn't need any diet remedies and reducing programs in those days.

We drank out of fruit jars (this is fashionable today in some restaurants), wore homemade flour sack shirts, and used kerosene lamps. We really had designer brands: "Red Head," "Buley Mills," and "Checkerboard."

In fact, Mama would not buy a sack of flour unless it had the potential of making a good shirt or some other article of clothing. We had no need for shoes except in cold weather, and we didn't eat T-bone steaks. Our menu consisted of wild rabbit, squirrel, quail, and, would you believe, possum! Mama had a special recipe for sweet potatoes and possum. The possum lay right in the center of the pan, head and all, and looked you right in the eye.

Granted, present-day niceties are wonderful, but you can get by with a lot less. I'm not suggesting that we all go back to the "good old days," but we can conserve and get by on considerably less if we really need to— especially for the purpose of getting out of debt.

It's foolish to weigh ourselves down with so much debt that we die from a heart attack, striving to be happy with things we cannot afford and could postpone. "The thrill now and the kill later."

One by-product of becoming debt free, even with the few sacrifices you may have to make, is the impression you will make upon your children. If you handle it right, your children will learn the value of money and how to be content with what they have. You can teach them the "attitude of gratitude" as they see you count your blessings. One of these days, your children will sit around their table talking with their children (your grandchildren) about the "good old days" when they ate "armadillo stew" and became financially independent!

How Am I Doing, Doc?

Once your plans are in place and your goals are set, semi-annual checkups are recommended. These checkups should cover (1) where you are now, (2) what progress has been made, and (3) any changes in your income and expenses. From these, determine if there are any changes that should be made in your plan.

In order to insure a healthy money tree and a secure future, checkups are a must. A small problem, left untended, can grow into a serious infection. But if detected early, a solution can usually be found.

As goods increase,
so do those who consume them.
And what benefit are they to the owner except
to feast his eyes on them?
— Ecclesiastes 5:11

CHAPTER TWENTY-FOUR

Savings and Investments: Where to Begin And What to Avoid

Plans fail for lack of counsel,
but with many advisers they succeed.
— Proverbs 15:22

The old saying, "save for a rainy day," still applies. If you don't save and invest for yourself, I doubt anyone else will do it for you. Everybody talks about savings, but few ever do anything about it.

As you begin your investment portfolio, there are some basic decisions you need to make and certain things that need to be in place. You need to make sure your assets are protected and that you have adequate coverage for calamities and the unexpected. Building bridges to span such events requires planning.

Savings and investments are vital—not only for now but also for retirement. You *will* grow old, unless you die before the proverbial "allotted time." One out of eight people in America will be over sixty-five by the year 2000, and health care costs will continue to rise. It has been estimated that they will triple over the next twenty years.

Savings are not only essential for you as an individual, but are vital in providing funds for investment in our nation's businesses and infrastructure, thus helping to insure that America can compete in today's growing global market.

We have not been a nation of savers, but of spenders. Japan's per capita savings far exceeds our own. It is no mystery that they have the money to buy our land, factories, and banks. We must change our course for the benefit of us all.

The longer you delay your savings and investment program, the more drastic the correction will have to be. It's like approaching a sharp curve in the road. Gradually easing into the curve is better than having to make a sharp turn at the last minute. There is finally a point where you cannot negotiate the turn. The same principle holds true in your investment portfolio. The sooner you start, the more "time" will work for you and the more productive it will be. The more time you have, the less money it takes. The typical procrastinator is always waiting for the "time to be right."

Insurance

Before beginning your investment plan, it is vital that you have your insurance in order. Protection for your possessions and security for your family should be considered first. Insurance is a tricky, risky business. There are all kinds of insurance policies. I might add that there are also all kinds of insurance salesmen who will gladly sell you insurance, not always in your best interest, but in theirs (big commissions). Young couples are prime targets. Always consult with a qualified and ethical insurance agent or broker for the proper coverage for all your insurance needs.

Health Insurance. A hospital stay for one major illness can rob you of all your assets. Health insurance is an absolute must.

Life Insurance. Your specific needs depend on the size of your family, your responsibilities, what you want to happen to your family, and any charitable giving you want to do. Caution: Do not break yourself trying to over-insure yourself. There is still a God in heaven who can sustain us. We do need to be aware, however, that calamities do come, and insurance will help bridge the financial gap. Buy insurance from companies rated A+ by A.M. Best, AA by Moody's, and AAA by Standard & Poor's.

Umbrella Liability Policy. The more wealth you have, the more the "buzzards" will circle overhead. If you have considerable assets, an umbrella liability policy will cover what your homeowner's policy does not.

The Best Insurance. The best "insurance policy" is *good health.* Establish a healthy lifestyle. Bad habits will cost you a fortune. Three prime examples are tobacco, alcohol, and drugs. They can rob you in a number of ways: (1) They cost you plenty, (2) they steal your savings, (3) they increase your doctor bills, (4) they can cause you to lose your job, (5) and they can bring untold misery to you and your family. The money saved by avoiding or giving up these habits can amount to a fortune. *"He who loves pleasure will become poor; whoever loves wine and oil will never be rich"* (Proverbs 21:17).

Your Savings Plan

Have you thought about how much you should set aside for savings? I suggest a minimum of 5 to 10 percent, depending on your income level. The 80-10-10 plan is a good one: 80 percent for your present needs, 10 percent for giving, and 10 percent for savings. By the way, a 10 percent giving plan does not cost you 10 percent since Uncle Sam allows you a charitable deduction. The tax savings can be as much as one-third of the contribution.

Your initial savings should be put into a liquid-type investment (such as a bank certificate of deposit) until you have at least a six-month cash reserve for emergencies. After that, begin your long-term investment plan.

Everyone's situation is different, so everyone's plan must be different. You can get information and help in making decisions about your savings plan from your employer, your local Social Security office, your accountant, your stock broker, your insurance agent, and your own records and files. There are also a number of good publications that deal with savings and retirement. Your local library is a valuable source for these.

Important Considerations

Take the time now to consider the following questions. Each of these questions has a bearing on the amount of money you will need to invest and will determine your savings strategy.

- How much will my children's college education cost?
- What will be my life expectancy at retirement?
- What expenses will continue after retirement?
- What might be my future medical needs?
- What debts will I still owe at retirement?
- What Social Security benefits should I expect to receive?
- What income can I expect from company profit sharing plans, IRA accounts, and other sources?

Now, get with your accountant or financial advisor and determine how much you will have to save each month so that you will have the funds you will need when you need them.

How Money Can Work For You

If putting aside money for savings seems too difficult, consider the following examples of how significant amounts of money can be accumulated if you spend wisely and save even small amounts.

- If at age twenty-five, you buy a house and borrow $75,000 for thirty years at 10½ percent interest and the payments are $686 per month, the house will ultimately cost $246,960 (360 payments of $686).

If instead, you get a twelve-year loan, the payment will be $918 per month and the house will cost $132,192 (144 payments of $918). You will save $114,768.

If you choose the twelve-year loan, and if, when the payments are complete, you continue to invest the amount of the house payment in a mutual fund that earns 12 percent per year for the next eighteen years, then when you are fifty-five years old, you will have $653,367 in the bank. At that point, if you stop putting in more money, the earnings will still continue to grow and your investment will be worth $2,029,259 at age sixty-five and $6,302,570 at age seventy-five. This is certainly a good way to buy a house!

• Let's say you save just $3.50 per day by not buying things like: cigarettes, soft drinks, and junk food. You will save $1,277 each year. Let's say you invest these "new-found" dollars and earn 12 percent per year. If you start this at age twenty-five, then at age sixty-five your investment will be worth $1,098,313. At the age of seventy-five, it will be worth $3,431,109!

• Let's say that at age twenty-five you refrain from buying one item you don't need that costs $500. Instead, you put that money into an IRA that earns 12 percent per year. In forty years, at age sixty-five, you will have $46,522, and at age seventy-five, you will have $144,385! If you put $500 in the IRA every year, at age sixty-five you will have $430,037, and at age seventy-five, you will have $1,343,425!

• Let's say you are twenty-five years old and you buy a car. To do so, you borrow $15,000 for sixty months at 10½ percent interest, and the payment is $322 per month. The total cost is $19,320 (60 payments of $322). Let's say that, instead, you buy a used car and borrow $7,500 for twenty-four months at 10½ percent interest.

The payments will be $348 per month and the total will be $8,352 (24 payments of $348), with a savings of $10,968!

● If your grandfather had put just $200 in an investment for you seventy-five years ago and it had earned 12 percent per year, today it would be worth $955,670. (I could kick Grandpaw for not doing just that one little thing for me.)

Get-Rich-Quick Schemes

In the next chapter we will talk about good investments. But now let's talk about a few things you should stay away from.

Who gets rich in a get-rich-quick scheme? Right, the schemer! Repeat with me, "If it sounds too good to be true, it probably is."

It's amazing how all these "no-way-to-lose deals" get dreamed up. Leave it to good old American ingenuity mixed in with a little greed and—bang—there it is. The prime targets for many of these schemes are the young and unsuspecting. However, no age group is exempt. The schemers have a scheme tailored for everyone.

The Great Pyramid Scheme

The old pyramid scheme has been around for ages, just dressed up in different clothes (designer clothes at that). There is not enough money in the world to fund these schemes. And there aren't enough people in the world to continue the pyramid's expanding base (if everyone is to make money).

Buying a boxcar load of possum traps (or anything else) so that you can sign up distributors to sell them to others just won't last. Pyramids are burial grounds—they leave the "down-level" investor buried under a garage full of possum traps.

Hurry, Hurry, Hurry!

"There are only two spots left, and you must act now!" This kind of statement is always a red flag. Actually, the best thing to do is leave those two spots and run out the back door.

Big Interest Bonus

Be leery of the promise of high interest rates and big returns on potential investments. I know several folks who lost their life savings because they invested in such scams.

The scenario usually goes like this: "If you give us just $10,000, we'll double your money in only 12 months." They say they will use the money in some big money-making investment, and thus will easily achieve such results. What they actually do is use the money they get from you to pay the high interest due the previous victims. They plan to get someone else to "loan" them more money so they can pay you your interest, and on it goes until they are unable to enlist anyone else. And all the while, they are skimming money off the top. If you are unlucky enough, you will be in the last group of investors and lose everything you put up. I had a dear friend, a retired school teacher, who lost his life's savings in such a scam—about $250,000. He died of a heart attack a few months later.

Not long ago, there was a timber scam that went like this: You loaned the promoter money with the promise of a very high interest rate. The promoter was supposedly buying timber rights on large tracts of land

and was to make a killing on future timber sales. Bankers, educators, businessmen, and everyday folks got caught up in the whirlwind. No one ever thought of checking up on what was really happening to their money. Results? You guessed it. The roof caved in, and the house of cards fell. When the dust settled, it was discovered that there was no timber to sell. The outcome for the investors? "Goodbye, Snowbird!"

The Commodity Futures Market

Beware! The Commodity Futures Market is like David versus Goliath, except that David doesn't have a sling shot and Goliath always wins. It's the individual versus the market and the large trading companies. The big boys can buy and sell in huge quantities and send prices tumbling or soaring in seconds, but by the time you hear about it, it's too late. Panic selling based on rumors or on the cancellation of some big foreign grain order can wipe you out in a few seconds. Then there are the futures "pit speculators" who are on the floor making split-second decisions. (This is why they pay such large fees for their seat at the exchange.) Then add a broker who has an incentive to churn your account (big commissions). With all this working against you, it's no surprise that most commodities investors lose their entire investment in no time at all. Someone has said that the only difference between Las Vegas and Chicago's LaSalle Street is the neon lights.

Beware of "Un-Real Estate" Scams

Back in the 1920s, a promoter sold unsuspecting New Yorkers thousands of acres of land and waterfront lots in the beautiful sunshine state of Florida. The problem was that most of the land was nonexistent, and the waterfront lots had water all right, but it was on *top* of the land.

Unsuspecting investors in recent years have been suckered into condo deals in which the promoter ran off with millions and left the investors owning the top floor—with no floors underneath! Beware of limited partnerships that promote such deals. There is a saying concerning partnerships: "At the beginning, the investor has the money and the manager has the experience; at the end, the manager has the money and the investor the experience." Billions of dollars have been lost by people who invested in highly-leveraged real estate deals.

Off-Shore Bank Scams

These fast-lane operators buy banks (usually offshore) and suck in depositors with the lure of high-interest rates. After all, banks are good, conservative institutions, aren't they? Well, not always. It depends on who runs the show. After they have pulled in millions and the fruit is ripe, they pick the tree of all the juicy apples and take off to the Riviera, leaving you with the cores.

Gold Mines

A sale of phony stock in a non-existent South African gold mine was promoted recently and brought in untold millions. In just one small Montana city, $15 million was extracted from "Gold Bug" citizens. The deal, oddly enough, sounded too good to be true. Repeat after me again: "If it sounds too good to be true, it probably is." The promoter who fronted the deal was a former mirror and tile installation man, suddenly turned "Gold Mine Expert."

A Revolving Door

Don't fall for these "investment" traps. My advise is to install a revolving door with a high-speed button so that when one of these schemers shows up, you can give him a fast spin back out the way he came in! If you don't have a revolving door, run out the back door, and if there's not a back door, make one!

Telephone Sales

Telephone salesmen may be inexperienced college kids or highly-trained professionals—either may get a large portion of your money. There are, of course, exceptions to all rules, but in 99 percent of the cases, you are in trouble if you buy over the telephone from someone you don't know. I'm speaking from experience here. I bit once, and I'm still looking for that rascal. The best advice I can give you is simply to say: "I'm sorry, but I don't accept solicitations over the telephone," and then hang up. That will end the pitch everytime.

Unsolicited Mail

Never invest with only the information gained from something you receive in the mail. After all, the promoter is not going to tell you all the pitfalls. There may be a few good investment ideas that come in the mail from good sources, but even then, call or write for more information. Check references, and always read the fine print.

Again, never make an investment by mail without extreme caution. Make sure you have all the facts; and, most of all, know the person you are dealing with. Generally, the best policy is: trash and burn!

Three Periods of a Person's Financial Life.

The Ideal:
- The preparation period—ages 1-24.
- The working period—ages 25-65.
- The golden period—ages 65-until.

The Truth of the Matter:
- The wanting period—ages 1-24.
- The spending period—ages 25-65.
- The crying period—ages 65-until.

---

*You've got to know when to hold' em
and know when to fold' em.*

CHAPTER TWENTY-FIVE

Investments to Consider

*Money talks. But all it says to
most people is "goodbye."*

Most people never realize that one of the hardest working "hands" is not actually at the workplace. He will work twenty-four hours a day. He never sleeps or eats. While you're sleeping, or even on vacation, he keeps on slaving for you. He is the best, most consistent earner you will ever have. He will collect for you and is full of energy. He will not pollute the environment. He is very smart, and he wants to go to work at once. It is a mystery that he has been so long neglected and mistreated. Everybody has this servant. His name is *money*. It is your job to put him to work.

Where to Put Your Money to Work
There are many different kinds of investments. The investment that is best for one person may not be best for you. It depends on your age, your disposition, your personal needs, and your plans for the future. In the next chapter we'll discuss investing in the stock market, but here I have listed a number of other investments you might consider.

Individual Retirement Account (IRA). Everyone should have an IRA. The tax deduction you obtain up front, plus the long-term benefits, make IRAs an ideal investment.

U. S. Treasury Obligations. These are good, safe investments that produce a steady income. When interest rates are high, the price of existing bond values will be relatively lower. When interest rates are low, existing bond values will be higher. Many investors try to buy during high-interest periods and sell when interest rates fall, thus reaping additional profits.

One type is Zero Coupon Bonds. These bonds are ideal for those who have funds to invest on a long-term basis or those who wish to speculate on falling interest rates. They are 100 percent guaranteed by the federal government and are bought at a deep discount, depending upon their maturity date and current interest rate. A $1,000 bond may cost as little as $150. Your principle and interest are not paid until maturity. However, the imputed interest is taxable each year. This makes them a great investment for IRAs and other tax-deferred retirement accounts. Should you prefer to hold the bonds to maturity, you can realize as much as eight times your investment, depending on the timing of your purchase and the maturity date of the bonds.

Money Market Funds. These are usually best for short-term liquidity purposes and can be very safe.

Tax-Free Municipal bonds. These are good for those in a high income tax bracket.

Certificates of Deposit. CDs are very safe up to $100,000. However, interest is usually relatively low.

Annuities. An annuity is a contract with an issuer to provide you with a series of payments at a future date based upon the amount of payments you make to the issuer. One advantage of an annuity is there is no current income tax on earnings so your money can grow at a faster rate. Annuities can be tailored to your particular needs. You can make lump sum contributions, regular monthly payments, or sporadic contributions depending on the issuer's policy. There are two basic kinds of annuities: the fixed and the variable. In the fixed annuity, the issuer guarantees you a fixed return. In a variable annuity, your money is invested by the issuer in a diversified stock, bond, or money market fund subject to market fluctuations. This can provide a greater return, but, of course, at a greater risk. There is no guarantee of the fund's performance.

Before investing in a annuity, check out the company and the contract.

Some important points to note:
- The historical performance of the management of the company
- All charges and commissions—both front-end and annual fees
- Withdrawal rights—penalty and surrender charges

Antiques and coins. These can be very risky. You must understand the business. These are not for the unsophisticated investor. Buy for pleasure. A profit motive should be secondary.

Precious Metals. You have two choices. You can buy the actual metal or you can buy stocks in companies that mine the metals. When you buy the metal, it must be stored in a safe place. When you buy the mining stocks, there can be dividends, and there is no charge for storage. These investments can be good in uncertain times. Many investors consider gold to be a safe haven and a good insurance policy against major crises.

Houses. A home is a good investment, but be sure that you are able to stay in the area for a reasonable period of time. Otherwise, it's best to rent. The advantage of owning your home is that instead of paying rent you are building equity, plus it may be possible to get some income taxes benefits. Old homes in a stable neighborhood sometimes make a good investment, especially if you have a knack for remodeling. Always shop carefully.

Rental Property. If you are a good repairman and can handle the headaches, rental property may be for you. If not, a limited partnership may be what you need. Location, good construction, and the right amenities are the key.

Vacant Land. This should be bought only in an area where there is real potential for future growth. Roads, shopping centers, and employment opportunities are very important. The Chamber of Commerce, the State Highway Department, and county and city agencies can give you valuable information.

I have had great success in buying several large tracts of land and dividing them into two- to five-acre lots. There are a large number of people who would like to build their homes on such lots just outside most every city. The key here is to purchase land that has easy access and a good road system already in place.

Small Businesses. There are many opportunities in small businesses, but you must be careful. You must be fully aware of what you are getting into!

If you buy an existing business, there are a few things you need to consider:

- Find out why they want to sell.
- Review their financial statements and federal income tax returns for the past five years. Was the company profitable? Were profits increasing or declining?
- Study their debt and determine exactly what you will be assuming. Are there any contingent liabilities?
- Determine the company's cash flow needs.
- Study their inventory. Are they overstocked? How old is the inventory? How much obsolete inventory is there? This is one area that can spell real trouble.
- Study their accounts receivables. There may be a lot on the books, but if much of it is past due, you may never collect it.
- Look carefully at their location. It is said that there are three important things in the retail business: location—location—location! Is there new highway construction planned that will affect the traffic flow to the business?
- Study all leases. You don't want to find after you take over that you have only a few months left or that the rent is just about to double.
- Check the condition of the building—especially the roof, plumbing, climate control, and other systems.
- Check the credit status with vendors. What payables will you be assuming? Is there a good relationship? You can also check the business' credit rating through one of the credit reporting agencies like Dun and Bradstreet.
- Check the reputation of the business in the community.
- Determine if there is a growing market for the company's products or services.

- Learn what the competition's strengths and weaknesses are. How do they affect this business?
- Determine if there is sufficient capital in the company or if you will have to put in more cash.
- Make sure you have the necessary knowledge and skills to properly run the business.
- Ask yourself if you are committed to the long hours required. (When you work for yourself, forget the clock.)
- Think about what you can do to improve on what the present management is doing.
- Consider the strengths and weaknesses of the company and its long-term prospects.

Nothing will ever be attempted
if all objections must be first overcome.
— Samuel Johnston

CHAPTER TWENTY-SIX

Understanding the
Stock Market

Whoever watches the wind will not plant;
whoever looks at the clouds will not reap.
— Ecclesiastes 11:4

The stock market can be a rewarding place to invest your money. But there are also many ways you can lose. It is crucial that you become well versed in its intricacies and know what you are doing before you invest.

The Bulls and the Bears

A bull market? A bear market? What are these? Their names are not too far from the truth. If you don't grab the bull by the horns, chances are you'll get eaten by the bears. One thing is sure, there's a lot of bull going on up there.

Very few investors fully understand the stock market. If you had a dozen experts together, their opinions would vary greatly. There are so many forces at work, all sending different signals to the market, that no one can predict tomorrow's rise or fall consistently. If you could, you would become a billionaire overnight.

In my opinion, the old investment philosophy of just buying one stock and holding it for twenty years is no longer wise. Sure, this has worked in some cases, and a few stocks can be cited to prove it, but that is 20/20 hindsight. You must be ready to change your position at any time.

The Changing Times

There are so many changes ahead—new technology, new industries, and new global markets. It will require expertise and persistence to get the most for your investment dollar. Past success is no guarantee for the future. *The past may be a good guidepost, but it is not a good hitching post.*

Investing in today's world has become very complicated. It can be rewarding for those who know how and dangerous for those who don't. I recommend you seek out a good, professional stockbroker before you invest. Please note that I said *good* stockbroker. Get references and check them out! Good, sound investment advice is of great value.

Why has investment strategy become so important in the past few years? A whole new world has opened up for investment. Twenty-four-hour global markets are now a reality and are at your fingertips. These have come about before our very eyes. To compete wisely in this world market requires sophisticated strategy. Old structures are crumbling and a new world order is emerging. For the first time in history, more nations are pulling together and supporting each other than ever before.

Today's instant means of communication has opened our world to investment opportunities unparalleled in history. Major events around the world have an instant effect on the stock market. What goes on in the United States, Japan, the Mid-East, and Europe affects the whole world. The rise or dip in unemployment, trade balances, congressional behavior, taxes, earthquakes, world competition, shortages, over-production, death, fear, uncertainty, good news, bad news, inflation, recession—all have a profound effect. The markets are super sensitive and are instantly impacted by even the slightest change of events. Your problem as an investor is that you have no control over these events and, in many cases, absolutely no warning. Does this destroy the opportunity for investors? No, on the contrary, it offers new opportunities everyday for those who are prepared to act. But it does make it critical that you have a good investment strategy and good counsel.

Investment Strategy

You must have a specific strategy that you follow consistently if you are to be successful in the stock market. A good professional broker can help you decide what strategy is best for you. There are a number to choose from. Depending on your circumstances, your goals, and your disposition, a specific strategy can be planned for you.

One good way to invest is called dollar-cost-averaging. This is where you decide to buy a specific dollar amount of a particular stock each month. The good thing about this is that you will buy more shares when the stock price is down and less shares when the price is up. In the long run, you will accumulate a large block of stock at a low average-price-per-share.

Industry Sectors

Stocks generally move together within an industry. For example, most stocks in the energy sector move up together when an energy crisis is evident. Even stocks in companies who are performing poorly can move up during these times. I call this the "tidal phenomenon." As the tide comes in, the motion is set and drives everything up with it. When the tide goes out, most stock in the same sector go down together. You may find that occasionally it is better to own a stock whose company is performing poorly but whose industry is in favor, than to have a good company's stock that is in a industry that is out of favor.

Beware

A little knowledge can be dangerous. We sometimes think we can become experts overnight. You'll be money ahead if you really prepare yourself. Study all you can and listen to the experts. Getting a "hot tip" from a well-meaning friend and acting on unprofessional advice can be disastrous!

A word of caution: Too many stockbrokers and investment agents have only their interest and your money at heart. Never buy investments over the phone from an unknown salesman who has the latest hot tip and newly discovered stock bargains—even if he works for a large, well-known Wall Street firm.

Investing in Common Stocks

The basic unit of investment in the stock market is the common stock. There are thousands to choose from and you must carefully evaluate any you consider.

Mutual funds are a good way to invest in common stocks. Mutual funds are managed by professional money managers and can many times do better than you as an individual. They are better able to stay on top of fast-breaking news events and can react quickly.

You will find mutual funds employing all types of investment strategies. Several will be just right for you. Evaluate a mutual fund in much the same way you would evaluate a single stock.

In evaluating a specific stock for a buying decision, consider the following:

- How good is the management of the company? What are their strengths and weaknesses?
- Is there a growing market for the company's products or services?
- What do company management and brokerage firm analysts think about the company's prospects?
- Has the company had consistent earnings increases in the past? What are the prospects for future earnings? Is its P/E ratio reasonable?
- How will competitors affect the company in the future?
- Are dividends paid? How much? What is the rate of return? How long have they been paying

dividends? What are the prospects that the dividends will continue and increase?

- Is the company jeopardizing its balance sheet by paying out too much in dividends? If this is the case, ultimately the value of the stock will be affected because the company is depleting its assets.
- Is the company's balance sheet strong? Do they have excessive debt?
- What is the relationship of the company's inventory to sales? If the company's inventory is rising faster than sales, this could be a sign that the company is headed for trouble.
- Are the company's receivables increasing faster than sales? If so, this could mean trouble with collections.
- What is the debt to equity ratio? If it is high compared to other companies in the same industry, you may want to look elsewhere.
- What are their expansion plans for the future?
- Is the company a leader in its industry?
- What is the future viability of the company and the industry it serves?

Most of this information can be obtained through your local broker or you can write the company for 10-K and annual reports.

You can also learn a lot by reading the business section of your local newspaper, the Wall Street Journal, and other business periodicals. Tune in to the nightly television business programs, such as "Moneyline," "Wall Street Week," and "Nightly Business News." Learn as much as you can about the markets in which you are investing.

Types of Common Stocks.

Dividend Stocks. You *can* have your ca
too. By selecting stocks in good companie:
dividends, you can have immediate incom.. ˌ
chance to participate in the growth of the company.

Growth Stocks. This is stock in a company that is
increasing in sales and profits faster than others in its
industry. Its growth is usually funded internally or with
debt. While the price of the stock may increase rapidly,
they usually pay little or no dividends.

Blue Chip Stocks. These are the old reliable
standbys—solid, profitable, and big, with top-notch
management. Many still have growth potential, yet the
price of the stock may not increase as rapidly as some
growth stocks. However, your investment is relatively
safe.

Specific Industry Recommendations

I believe the following industries could be big winners
in the coming decade. But don't forget, there are both
good and bad performers in every industry.

The Energy Industry. World energy consumption is
certain to increase as the Third World nations become
more industrialized and as affluence spreads. Natural
resources are being depleted and alternate sources of
energy must be found to supply the world's needs.
Usually, energy stocks rise when energy supplies fall or
when threats to supplies exist. The long-term outlook is
generally good because of our limited amount of natural
resources. Be very careful about investing in oil and gas
exploration deals. Unless you can afford to lose your
entire investment, stay away. Murphy's Law works
overtime in the oilfield. Only a small number of wells

that are drilled are successful. Should you want to participate in oil and gas drilling, it's best to buy into a limited partnership. This way, the risk is spread over a number of prospects and investors. The quality of the partnership is based on the company that puts the partnership together. Many of the major oil companies do a portion of their drilling through these partnerships, and most major investment brokerage firms offer them. Be cautious, however, when it comes to private, limited partnerships. Know the principles and the prospects before you invest.

Waste Handling and Environmental Industry. More and more demand will be placed on government, business, and individuals to clean up our environment and keep it a safe place to live. The companies involved in waste disposal and environmental cleanup could be big winners.

Health Care Industry. Science and medical technology are advancing at a rapid rate. This will add to the life expectancy of every person. The fastest growing segment of society is sixty-five years and older. These factors will create additional demands on providing quality health care. Companies involved with health care stand to gain greatly.

Understanding the Lingo

It is important to learn the language of the stock market. Your understanding of the basic street talk is essential.

In the following glossary, I do not attempt to cover all the many variations and the more complex investment terms, but merely to provide a basic list. This should give you adequate information to begin your understanding of the stock market.

Glossary

Annual Report - A report to the shareholders about the condition of the company, along with a balance sheet, earnings, and other data important to the shareholders.

Ask Price - The price sellers are asking for their stock.

Bid Price - The price at which buyers are willing to purchase a stock.

Bear Market - A term used to describe the market that has been going down for some time. During these periods, most investors think that the prospects for the economy are not good; thus, sellers outnumber buyers, resulting in a down market.

Bond - A promissory note representing a debt owed by the issuer, with a specific interest rate and principle due on a specific date.

Blue Chip Stock - The stock of a top-rated, large company with a long-proven history of profits and stability.

Blue Sky Laws - Laws that govern the issuance of stock by corporations to protect investors from untrue claims, promises of "pie in the sky," and fraudulent statements.

Book Value - The value of a stock determined from a company's accounting records. This is determined by adding all assets and subtracting all debts and other liabilities. Note: Book value per share may be quite different from market value per share due to a number of factors, including future prospects, favorable and unfavorable press, and industry perceptions.

Broker - An agent who sells stocks and other securities.

Bull Market - The opposite of bear market. It is a time when investors believe the prospects for the market are good, so buyers outnumber sellers and push the market upward for an extended period of time.

Call - The option to buy a stock at a stated price per share within a certain period of time. The opposite of a put.

Capital Market - A market that deals in securities of both debt and equity.

Capital Stock - All the shares issued by a company that represent ownership.

Certificate of Deposit (CD) - A promissory note issued by a banking institution, usually insured to $100,000 by the federal government, with a stipulated interest rate and maturity date.

Common Stock - The most basic ownership interest in a corporation. Common stockholders own the equity in the company. They take the first risk of corporate ownership and expect the largest return for their investment if the corporation prospers.

Convertible Stock - Preferred shares or debentures that are convertible into common shares at a stipulated conversion price.

Corporate Bond - A promissory note issued by a corporation with a specific interest rate for a specific period of time.

Coupon - A coupon attached to a bond, which may be clipped on each due date and presented for payment of interest.

Debenture - Similar to a bond issued by a corporation to raise capital with specific rights stipulated.

Dividend - A payment of company earnings to each shareholder on a per share basis and approved by the company's board of directors.

Dow-Jones Average - A widely-quoted stock market average computed daily and based on thirty industrial company stocks.

Floor Broker - One who executes stock orders on the floor of the exchange.

Good Until Cancelled Order - An order to buy or sell that remains in place until filled or cancelled.

Growth Fund - A mutual fund whose goal is to increase its capital base by buying stocks with good prospects for increasing value quickly rather than buying stocks with large dividends and bonds paying current interest income.

Listed Stock - Stock that is traded on one of the security exchanges.

Margin - Buying stock and using it as collateral to borrow money to buy more stock.

Margin Call - A demand by the brokerage firm to put up additional cash when the market value of the stock falls below the allowable margin level.

Municipal Bond - A bond that is issued by a state or political subdivision rather than by the U.S. government or corporation.

Mutual Fund - A fund established by an investment company that offers shares to the public in a fund composed of stocks and/or bonds from a variety of companies and political subdivisions.

NASDAQ - The initials for the National Association of Security Dealers Automated Quotations system. This network provides dealers, brokers, and customers with price quotations on securities traded "over-the-counter."

NYSE Common Stock Index - A composite index showing the average value of all stocks listed on the New York Stock Exchange. This index is computed continuously and is available at any point during the day.

Odd Lot - Shares bought or sold that are in less than 100 share blocks.

Over-the-Counter (OTC) - A market for securities that are not listed on the exchanges, made up of thousands of companies.

Paper Profit - Unrealized profit on an investment before it is sold, based on the present quote.

Penny Stocks - Low price stocks, usually selling for less than a dollar. Usually very risky.

Point - The meaning depends on the subject discussed. A point is equivalent to one dollar when speaking of a stock price. In the case of bonds, a point equals ten dollars. A point, when speaking of the Dow, is simply a point in the Dow average and is not equivalent to any denomination. (Example: If the Dow yesterday was 2703.52 and today it is 2707.33, it is said that "the Dow went up four points today." It is typically rounded off to the nearest point in conversation.)

Price-Earnings Ratio (P/E) - The price of a share of stock as it relates to its earnings per share. Usually based on the previous twelve-month period. However, future earnings also are projected to estimate a future price-earnings ratio. This is used as one criterion for evaluating a stock. Example: A stock selling for twenty dollars a share that earned two dollars per share in the last twelve months is said to have a P/E ratio of ten.

Prospectus - A document required by the SEC that contains information about a new offering of securities for sale.

Proxy - A written authorization to allow someone else to vote your shares of stock at a stockholder's meeting.

Put - An option to sell a certain amount of shares at a definite price for a stipulated period of time. The opposite of a call.

Portfolio - All of the stocks and other securities that you own at any particular time.

Private Company - A company that is owned by private individuals and whose shares have not been offered for sale to the general public.

Public Company - A company that has sold shares to the general public and has registered with the SEC.

Quotation - A quote of the most recent price a buyer would buy and a seller would sell a stock for.

Rally - A brisk recovery following a decline in the market.

Red Herring - A preliminary prospectus sent out to prospective buyers in order to get an indication of the interest in a particular new issue of stock.

SEC - The initials for the Securities and Exchange Commission, which was established by Congress in 1933 to enforce security laws and designed to protect investors.

Sinking Fund - A fund set aside on a regular basis by a company in order to meet obligations for the redemption of preferred stock debentures, bonds, or other indebtedness.

Speculator - One that takes unusual risks in the markets, in hopes of making a quick profit.

Spread - The difference between the bid price and the ask price.

Stock Dividend - Additional shares are issued to each stockholder instead of cash.

Stock Exchange - An organization established for the purpose of buying and selling securities in an orderly market.

Stockholder of Record - A person whose name appears on the record books of a corporation as the holder of a specific number of shares of stock in the company.

Stock Split - When a company increases its outstanding shares. Example: A two for one split is when you receive one additional share for every share you own. Splits are used to increase the number of outstanding shares. More shares are then available for trading purposes at a lower price in hopes that more investors will be interested. A split does not change the percentage of ownership of any stockholder.

Street Name - Securities held in the name of a brokerage firm rather than in the stockholder's own name.

Transfer Agent - A firm that keeps the record for a company of its shareholders, including their names, addresses, and the number of shares held. They also issue new certificates and cancel old certificates as the securities are traded.

Treasury Bill - U.S. government short-term notes. Sold at competitive bids and maturing in thirteen weeks, twenty-six weeks, and one year.

Treasury Bond - U.S. government obligations which mature in ten years or longer.

Treasury Note - U.S. government obligations that mature in two to ten years.

Treasury Stock - Stock that was issued by the company and later reacquired. It may be held indefinitely, retired, or reissued to the public. Treasury Stock receives no dividends and has no voting rights.

Underwriter's Fee - The fee received by the investment banker or brokerage firm in arranging for a public or private offering of stock.

Unlisted Stock - A stock that is not listed on one of the exchanges.

Wall Street - The financial center of the U.S. stock markets located in New York City.

Warrant - A certificate issued giving the holder the right to purchase a security at a stipulated price, by a given date.

X Dividend - The day after a dividend is paid. If you buy the stock on that date, you will not be entitled to a dividend until the next one is declared.

Yield - The percent of return received from a dividend as it relates to the price of the stock. Example: A stock that has a current price of ten dollars per share and pays one dollar per share in dividends would have a 10 percent yield.

The 10 Mistakes Most Frequently Made by Investors

1. *No investment goal or purpose*
   You need to have a goal for your investments. What are you trying to accomplish? What are your needs? What time frame do you have to work with?

2. *Following the advice of friends instead of professional people*
   It is risky to follow the advice of friends. Check out the facts and seek out professional advice. The money you will save will be your own.

3. *Having a short-term view*
   You will generally fair much better if you go for the long term. Short term is always more risky in the stock market.

4. *Failure to diversify*
   Strive for a balance rather than placing all your money in one stock. There is safety in numbers. While one stock may not do so well, others may exceed your expectations.

5. *Fear of the ups and downs in the market place*
   Don't panic and sell when the market takes a dip. It has never failed to bounce back yet.

6. *Waiting for the right time*
   Investing is simple: "Buy low, sell high"! The problem is that you cannot consistently predict optimal timing. Invest regularly and with professional advice.

7. *Being unwilling to admit a mistake and holding on until the stock is worthless*
   If a stock has gone sour and the fundamentals of the company have changed, then the sooner you sell, the less you will lose.

8. *Investing in fads and long shots*
   While there may be a rare hit; 99 times out of 100, you will strike out.

9. *Failure to keep abreast of the investment climate and changing times and products*
   Know the market, your investment, and its industry sector—their trends, future prospects, and potential.

10. *Being greedy or impatient*
    Ignoring professional advice or market signals and holding onto a stock too long because of greed for "just a little more profit" can make you miss the boat altogether. On the other hand, being impatient and selling a good stock too soon rather than letting your profits run can be counterproductive.

A real good day at the market is when you and your wife spend the whole day at the mall and she finds nothing she likes.

CHAPTER TWENTY-SEVEN

How Do You Spell Success?

Before God's footstool to confess,
a poor soul knelt and
bowed his head. "I failed," he wailed.
The master said, "Thou
did'st thy best, that is success"
— Author unknown

Jim Corbett, the great boxer, gives this recipe for success: "Fight one more round. When your feet are so tired you have to shuffle back to the center of the ring, fight one more round. When your arms are so tired that you can hardly lift your hands, fight one more round. When your nose is bleeding and your eyes are black and you are so tired that you wish your opponent would crack you one on the jaw and put you to sleep, fight one more round—remembering that the man who always fights one more round is never whipped."

It Just Takes Luck!

There are few jobs in which ability alone is enough. Luck sometimes plays a part. If you want to succeed by luck, just do the following:

- Have a pleasing personality: positive, cooperative, kind, sincere, loyal, enthusiastic, and courteous.
- Perform your work consistently and thoroughly.
- Listen and learn.
- Always be on time and stay until the job is done.
- Don't offer excuses and never blame others.
- Be a producer and not just a consumer.

Lessons from the Hounds

I learned early in life that being busy did not necessarily bring success.

We had two hunting dogs. One was named Skinner. Ol' Skinner could sniff out a rabbit in no time flat. You could always count on Ol' Skinner. A real winner who always helped us find rabbit for supper!

We were mighty proud of Skinner's hunting skills. He became the standard we compared our other dogs to.

We also had another dog, and for the life of me, I can't remember his name, so I'll just call him "Ol' Rip." (Isn't it interesting that we always forget the names of losers.)

Ol' Rip could sniff out a hot track just as fast as Skinner and would soon give that familiar bark. We would beat our way through the woods to the spot. When we got there, Skinner would be lying nearby— half asleep and looking bored—while Rip would be wildly digging in the ground, sniffing, growling, and slinging dirt out of the hole by the bucketfuls, until he had dug himself out of sight. Finally out of the hole would come a small helpless mouse. Little comfort for boys who were expecting rabbit stew for supper. All that effort for naught.

Well, we never did break Ol' Rip of his enthusiasm for digging up mice. He sure would be proud of all his two-legged buddies, who are still wasting time "chasing mice" today and never find real success.

Follow-Through

If you are to have success in any endeavor, you must be able to follow through on your ideas. Dreams and hopes are the beginning of success, but follow-through brings them to reality.

Please don't get caught in what I call the "I hope trap." Many dreams never get past the hope stage. Most people's hope box is filled up and running over. Here is a typical "hope" conversation:

"I hear you want to start your own business."

"I sure hope to."

"Well, when do you plan to get started?"

"I hope to start real soon."

"When will you have your plans completed?"

"Well, I hope, before very long."

"Do you think you can get it going by this time next year?"

"I sure hope so."

"I understand it will only require a small amount of capital to finance."

"That's what I'm hoping."

"I understand also that all your family will chip in and help work in the business."

"Well, I sure hope so."

"I overheard your wife saying that she would be handling all the money."

"My goodness, alive, I sure hope not!"

Hopes and dreams are great; in fact, this is where success begins, but without follow-through, your dreams will not come true.

Success in a Nutshell

Success can be bought like any commodity. The only difference is that it must be bought on the long-term installment plan.

1st payment—Be ethical. There are no shortcuts or substitutes.

2nd payment—You must work hard and manage your time well.

3rd payment—Be totally committed. Never, never, never give up.

4th payment—Be prepared. Know yourself and your job.

5th payment—Make sure your timing is right. If the ship has pulled out, find another one; if it is sinking, get off and get on another one.

6th payment—Control your spending habits.

A Rise To Fame

There are few that rise to fame and early success, but it does happen. A friend of mine signed up as a shoe dealer for a mail-order, shoe-manufacturing company. Recently he received the following certificate (along with an appropriate bumper sticker):

𝕮𝖔𝖓𝖌𝖗𝖆𝖙𝖚𝖑𝖆𝖙𝖎𝖔𝖓𝖘, 𝕵.𝕮.!

𝔜𝔬𝔲𝔯 𝔭𝔢𝔯𝔣𝔬𝔯𝔪𝔞𝔫𝔠𝔢 𝔡𝔲𝔯𝔦𝔫𝔤 𝔱𝔥𝔢 𝔭𝔞𝔰𝔱 𝔶𝔢𝔞𝔯 𝔦𝔰 𝔳𝔞𝔩𝔲𝔢𝔡 𝔞𝔫𝔡 𝔞𝔭𝔭𝔯𝔢𝔠𝔦𝔞𝔱𝔢𝔡.
𝔜𝔬𝔲 𝔥𝔞𝔳𝔢 𝔟𝔢𝔢𝔫 𝔰𝔢𝔩𝔢𝔠𝔱𝔢𝔡 𝔞𝔰 𝔬𝔲𝔯

"𝕯𝖊𝖆𝖑𝖊𝖗 𝖔𝖋 𝖙𝖍𝖊 𝖄𝖊𝖆𝖗"

While being selected as "Dealer of the Year" was appreciated, it came as a complete surprise, as J.C. had only sold one pair of shoes during the entire year and he had sold that pair to himself!

Persistence

Back in the 1890s, a fourteen-year-old boy, who had just lost his father, sat down and tried to figure out how to get a job to care for himself and his family. Having only an eighth-grade education did not help much. He applied as an office boy to four different firms and was told by each one that they did not have enough work to keep him busy.

He pondered his predicament and then went back to the four firms. He offered each of them one-fourth of an office boy for one dollar a week. All four firms gave him a job.

This young lad's name was Emmett J. McCormack, who later became the co-founder of Moore-McCormack Lines, the second-largest American shipping company. Persistence and a little ingenuity made the difference.

Always Do a Little More and Then Some

Two girls worked in a candy store where they sold loose candy by weight. The boss noticed that one girl always had a line at her window whereas the other girl had very few or no customers. He could not understand the reason and asked the candy girl with the long line why this was so. She replied, "It's very simple. The other girl always puts too much candy on her scales and has to rake some off. I put on less than I need and have to add more." Which kind of person are you?

The Mother of Invention

Homemakers and butchers are indebted to an old candlestick maker. He worked in the New York City Candle Works around the turn of the century.

On his way home from work, he frequently stopped at a particular market to buy fish. It was always wrapped in ordinary paper. Long before he reached home, his package would be smelly, soggy, and offensive to his fellow trolley passengers. They complained, often very bitterly. One day, the candlestick maker took some paper to work and dipped it into molten wax. That night he wrapped his fish in this specially treated paper. There were no leaks, no odors, and no complaints. Wax paper was born. Necessity is the mother of invention.

A Brush With Success

A shy, country boy who could hardly read would not seem like a candidate for success. In his early twenties, he was dismissed from his first three jobs. However, he had one major thing going for him. He refused to give up. He began making brushes and sold them from door to door. Persistence and hard work eventually paid off. His name was Alfred C. Fuller, founder of the Fuller Brush Company, one of the largest direct-marketing companies in the United States.

A Clean Sweep

Murray Spangler, a store janitor in Canton, Ohio, had a terrible time sweeping the floors because the dust made him sneeze and cough. Most people would have given up and found another job. Instead, Spangler began to experiment to find a better way to clean floors.

He wanted to make something that didn't just push the dust around. Spangler's determination soon led to a workable, though crude, vacuum cleaner. He introduced it to an old friend in the leather business. The friend's name was H. W. Hoover. Perhaps you have one of Spangler's inventions in your home.

Just Sing

Some of you may be thinking, "My chance for success has come and gone. It's too late for me. Life has dealt me a heavy burden and the clock of time is about to run out."

Well, it all depends on how you spell success! Let me tell you the following success story.

An ordinary-looking package was delivered to my office and inside were two cassettes of gospel songs. I occasionally receive tapes from people hoping to get a song published. This one, however, was different. There was no request for me to buy or publish anything. It was just a gift!

The cassettes were obviously unprofessional. They were homemade and recorded on poor equipment. The singer would never make the "Top 40" (or 500) list or qualify for a part in a chorus. His voice at times would break and his organ accompaniment missed a few keys, but his spirit and enthusiasm came through loud and clear. He touched my heart with his singing.

You see, "Bill," like so many, had lost the strength of youth. He had passed into old age and was now looking into the sunset. Life had dealt Bill a cruel blow—he had lost both legs by amputation due to diabetes. However, Bill did not give up easily.

He bought himself an organ and hung a harmonica around his neck. Now he rolls himself up to the organ in his wheelchair and spends his time *just singing* and recording. Bill has even devised a way to add another sound track to harmonize with himself after he sings the lead part of the song.

So what do you do when life deals you a bad hand? Well, you *just sing* and keep going.

Is this not what David did when things got rough for him? King Saul sent out his army to kill him; he lost his best friend, Jonathan; and his rebellious son Absalom was killed. Read the Psalms and you'll find out what he did: He *just sang*!

Maybe, you too, like Bill or David, in such times, need to *just sing*.

The True Blessing of Success

The true blessing of success is the joy of managing God's business and meeting the needs of our own families and the less fortunate. We need to constantly pray for wisdom to use what we have to the best of our ability and to God's glory. After all, true success is not measured in dollars, but by the more important yardstick of character and servanthood.

There is a fine line between success and failure. It's like standing on a fence—a little push either way will cause you to fall on one side or the other. So it is in life. As the poet said, "One ship sails east, another sails west, by the self-same wind that blows; 'tis not the wind, but the set of the sails that determines which way she goes!"

Let no man worry about the success of his efforts. If he will perform each day to the best he can the work which is before him, he will wake up one day and find himself one of the competent ones of his generation.
— William James

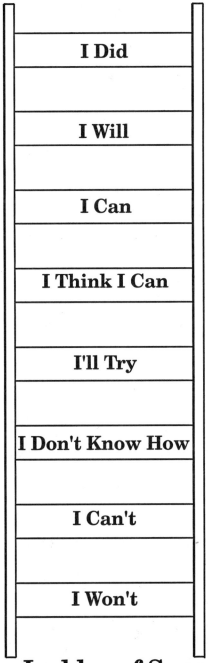

The Ladder of Success

CHAPTER TWENTY-EIGHT

Teach Your Children Well

Train a child in the way he should go,
and when he is old he will not turn from it.
— Proverbs 22:6

When one of my girls was very little, I told her we did not have the money to buy something she wanted. Her solution was simple: "Just write a check, Daddy."

Children need to be taught an accurate concept of how money works. But your actions speak louder than your words. If your debt is out-of-control, it will rob you of the joy of teaching your children how to properly manage money. If you are a poor money manager, what you try to teach your kids verbally will not be heard. As you get your spending under control, you can teach your children many valuable lessons. The best time to teach these lessons is in the early formative years. Without these important lessons, your children will grow up, to a large degree, financially ignorant and, in too many cases, totally irresponsible.

How Children See Money

"Little Ryan" begins to learn about money when he gets his first quarter and buys his own snow cone. His excitement is evident when he marches up to the counter and announces his favorite flavor.

You may remember when a gift of a dime was as good as a $100 bill to "little Callie"—it was all money to her little mind. Those exciting times soon become the "good old days" because, my, my, how their view of money changes by the time they reach ten.

When my first granddaughter, Korie, was about four years old, her favorite thing was to go with Papaw to buy an "Icee." Every convenience store that sold them were on her "little map." We were in the car one day, and I asked her what she would do if I gave her $1,000. I'll never forget her response, "I'd buy me Icees."

I can still recall when I was about six years old, some sixty years ago, when my great uncle John would visit our family. He would stand by the fireplace and reach into his pocket and pull out a penny and rub it on his pants leg. This would go on for what seemed like an hour, while we boys watched and wished. Finally, after all the polishing and waiting, he would hand us a bright, shiny penny that you could see your face in.

We could hardly wait for the next time Uncle John would come to see us. What an impression one little penny made on us. But don't try this today, as I doubt that a penny will satisfy Junior. He is already used to the "green" stuff!

The Mystery of Money

Children are so curious and impressionable. They grow up from the cradle observing how money works.

- They hear it "ping" as it hits the floor.
- They listen to it jingle in their pockets.

- They watch Mom and Dad stand in line for the privilege of "giving" it away to the person behind the counter.
- They see Mom and Dad write a note on paper (check) and exchange it for a toy.
- They go with Mom and Dad to the bank, where they evidently make the stuff.
- They hear Mom and Dad fight over it.
- They learn to sweep the floor and turn the sofa upside down to find some.
- They see Mom and Dad sell something to get it.
- They notice that the doctor won't get you well without some of it.
- They know the tooth fairy gives it to them for their teeth.
- They know Santa Claus puts it in their stocking.
- They observe that their parents have to give some to the preacher (obviously, to get him to stop preaching so they can go to McDonald's!).

My, my, what a mystery is this stuff called money, and what miracles it will work for you. Little wonder they grow up craving it!

Teaching the Basics

Parents, don't miss the opportunity to teach the basic lessons of money management in the formative days. If you will teach your children well, they will someday be ready to face life responsibly, and you will be left with a memory box full of wonderful memories.

The following suggestions, though simple, are fundamental in teaching your children the true value of money. It will fill your heart with joy to share these lessons with your little ones. These suggestions are so fundamental and simple that I almost hesitate to mention them. But as basic as they are, they are neglected by many parents.

Counting Money

The first lesson to teach your child is how to count money. It's fun to watch them master the different names of the coins and their value. Your memory box will be filled with memories of little eyes that light up with expressions of confidence when they discover that they can tell the difference in all those pieces of money.

Piggybanks

Encourage your children to save some of their money. No matter how young, they will learn valuable lessons and gain a great sense of accomplishment when they see how much they have accumulated and are then able to buy something special for themselves or someone they love. As they get older, open a savings account for them so they can learn the value of compound interest.

Working for Money

Children need to know that Dad and Mom have to work for money. Explain to them how work is transferred into money, and that everybody has to "pitch in" and work in order to buy things. Teach them that when they waste money, they waste their work and energy.

Value of Goods

While shopping with your children, point out the differences in the prices of things you see. Explain why one item is so much more expensive than another item on the same shelf.

The History and Purpose of Money

Explain that before money was used, people traded something they had for something they wanted. They might trade ten goats for a horse or two bushels of corn for a chicken. Teach them that value was established on the basis of how much work was involved in raising the animals or growing the produce. Eventually, people decided to make coins and paper money to represent the worth of work, animals, food, etc. These were easier to carry around, and they could be hidden or put into banks for safe keeping until needed.

How Checks Work

Explain that writing checks draws from the money we have asked the bank to keep for us. When we write a check, we are simply telling the bank to let someone else have some of our money. This may sound elementary, but not to your child. Children believe that as long as you have checks, you can buy anything you want! Why would they ever think such a thing? Very simple, they have watched you write checks for things you want all their "little lives." If they don't learn these

lessons while they are young, don't be surprised if, as
adults, they have serious problems with overdrafts.

Family Time

Play money games with your children that teach how
money works. There are a number of such games on the
market that are fun, as well as educational.

Allowances

Children should receive allowances, if for no other
reason, than because they have needs; and what you
earn for the family is partly to meet those needs. In
addition, having their own money to spend teaches
them how to be good money managers. Make them
responsible for buying some specific needed items with
their allowance, like school lunches. They should also be
given enough to make some personal buying decisions.
They need to buy Christmas and birthday gifts for
others with their allowance. Teach them to be good
stewards and to give some to God. When they get older,
open a checking account for them and teach them to use
it responsibly. Teach them to reconcile their statement
every month. It is sad to see so many adults who don't
know how to do this. Lastly, teach them the value of
saving. That piggybank is very important and a savings
account in the teenage years will give them a sense of
pride and accomplishment. Through these learning
experiences, they will become the good money managers
you want them to be.

Chores

Every child should have chores that are simply their
contribution to the household. Chores teach
responsibility and that they must contribute to the
overall needs of the family. They should also be given
jobs over and above their regular chores to earn extra

money. This teaches them that you earn money by working. They learn that money is not free. They begin to understand that when they waste money on foolish things, they are really wasting their work reward. If you have teenagers, you will notice that they are much less prone to drive all over town if they have to buy their own gas!

The Proper Use of Money

Teach your children how to use their money properly. Money provides us with our basic necessities—food, clothing, and a house to live in. Teach them that giving and sharing is also an important part of using money properly. Wasting money on bad habits will not only leave them without money, but will destroy their good health, which enables them to earn money.

By teaching them the principles in this book, you will be building a foundation for financial responsibility that will support them throughout their lives. Instill in them the proper view of wealth, so that money, for the sake of money, will not become their sole aim in life and their "god."

These simple principles are vital and *must* be taught to your children. The joy you will receive will fill your memory box to overflowing and . . . "your children will rise up and call you blessed" (Proverbs 31:28).

The surest way to teach children to count is to distribute their gifts unevenly.

CHAPTER TWENTY-NINE

Wills—Whose Shall It Be?

But God said to him, "You fool!
This very night your life will be
demanded from you. Then who will get
what you have prepared for yourself?"
— Luke 12:20

"Of all the sad words of tongue or pen, the saddest are these: 'It might have been'" (Whittier).

How many fortunes have been left to be spent by lawyers for endless legal work trying to untangle a big mess? Families break-up, hard feelings result, relatives never speak to each other again, children are left without care or direction, even murders occur—all because the deceased did not leave a will. About seven out of ten people die without a will. This is a shame.

Uncle Joe's Funeral

Strange people often show up at a rich uncle's funeral: folks the family hasn't heard from in thirty years. They're all "broken-hearted" and so concerned about "dear old Uncle John . . . uhm . . . or was his name Joe?" And they're wondering all the time how much he left. I can tell you one thing for sure, he left it all.

You may have read about James Meadow, the man who died leaving a multi-billion dollar fortune in the Spindle Top Texas oilfield and no will. Well, my wife's maiden name is Meador, and she was a relative of dear old Uncle James. (Her branch of the family changed the spelling.) The first problem, according to the newspaper articles, is that they don't know where all the money is. The next problem is that thousands of dear old Uncle James' nieces, nephews, and cousins have come forward, claiming to be his descendants. At this point, there are volumes of court records. Research is being done to trace down all his descendants to determine who is supposed to get all the money and where it all is. I have cautioned my wife not to send dear old Uncle James any belated flowers or spend any of this fortune until she sees it in our bank account.

Dearly Beloved

The heirs sat reverently and expectantly. The attorney slowly began to read "rich" Uncle Conrad's will. "Dearly Beloved: I Conrad B. Smith, in the presence of witnesses herein, being of sound mind, keen judgement, and knowing you all full well, do solemnly declare that I spent it all."

A Jar of Pennies

A new highway was being built in Texas when it was discovered that it went right through the middle of an old graveyard. The contractor was finally given permission to move the graveyard to a new location, which was quite an "undertaking." In the digging, they found a fruit jar full of pennies. For years, the jar had been lying next to the deceased's bony fingers, and the amazing thing was that he hadn't spent a penny of it!

Many have tried to "take it with them," but no one has figured out how to use it. The Pharoahs and the American Indians tried it, all to no avail. Have you ever seen a hearse pulling a U-Haul on the way to the cemetery? If you ever do, tip your hat, because the deceased must have been a real optimist!

A Will Is a Must

It is very important to provide for your family after your death. In fact, the Bible encourages it. How much will they need? What portion should I leave to God's work? Who will get what is left? These are soul-searching questions that need to be answered and re-answered as you grow older and as your needs and your family's needs change. One of the tragic things of life is that many never sit down and analyze such things and never prepare a will so that their wealth can be properly used after they are gone.

What Will Happen?

If you have no will, here is what can happen: The state can take charge. Your small children may be placed in a home that you would not approve of. You can count on a fight among relatives, unless you are a pauper. (The bigger the pot, the more the relatives.) If there are no relatives, then the state takes it all. If your affairs are left in complicated entanglements without direction, lawyer fees will eat up a large portion.

Decision Time

How do you decide who will receive your estate? This is a most important question, and one that too few give serious thought to. Remember, no decision is a decision. If you make no decision, the decision you have made is to leave it to the state and lawyers to decide.

What profit is your lifetime of work and your diligent saving if it is squandered by those who oppose all you believe? After all, your wealth has been accumulated with God's help, and you should make careful decisions concerning its disposition.

When deciding who to leave your wealth to, take a good look at the lives of the possible beneficiaries. Consider their lifestyles. Are they responsible and able to handle money? What about their ethical and moral standards?

I have known some who have left their estate to irresponsible children and it has only hastened disaster in the lives of the recipients.

How About God?

As a Christian, I certainly do not want to leave God's kingdom work out of my will. Why should I change the giving pattern I have practiced all my life?

In fact, as Christians, do we not believe that in death we come into the presence of God, our creator? At the very point when I will give an account of my stewardship, how contradictory to say, "Sorry, God, you were left out of my future plans!" How much more fitting to be able to say, "Lord, I gave a portion to good works, and I left the rest of what you entrusted to me to those who will carry on your work until you require it of them."

Tax Planning

Tax planning is a vital part of your will. There are many ways to lessen the tax bite with proper planning. Through gifts, trusts, and insurance, you can protect and increase your estate. The laws in this area are complicated, so seek good, professional advice for your specific situation.

Updating Your Will

If you have already made your will, Congratulations! However, if you have not updated it for some time, it is a must that you do so.

Keeping a will up to date is as important in writing one in the first place. Listed below is a check list of things to consider in updating your will:

- Have you moved? Every state has different laws that govern the settling of estates. You need to make certain your will is in compliance with the laws of your state.
- Have you had a change in marital status? If so, you may want to rethink your prior decisions.
- Have you acquired property in other states? Check the laws in those states, your will may need to be modified.
- Have you had a change in your family make up? New arrivals need to be considered, as well as deaths or marriages of your children.
- Have your children grown to independence? Their needs change and you may need to make modifications. You no longer need to be concerned about their education, their guardianship, etc.
- Have your financial circumstances changed? You may have sold a number of assets or made lifetime gifts to reduce any estate taxes. If so, your will may need to be modified.
- Is your executor still able to serve? He or she may have died or for some other reason can't act for you as planned.
- If you have young children, is the person you have designated as guardian upon your death still willing and able to serve?

These are just some of the reasons that it is important to review your will periodically. Tax laws are constantly being changed by the federal and state government. Do not attempt to make these changes yourself. Have a qualified attorney help you decide what changes must be made.

Final Advice

Sit down and determine what you have by drawing up a list of your assets. Determine how and to whom you want to leave your estate. With this information, seek out a good lawyer who can appreciate your purposes and have him help you draw up your will.

Never purchase a will packet through mail order advertisements. They cannot possibly take into consideration all the situations people find themselves in. And never try to write a will yourself. The laws are complicated and change often. The small lawyer's fee will save your heirs many headaches and, most of all, will allow your wealth to continue to work after you are gone in the way that you would desire.

After a long time the master of those servants returned and settled accounts with them. The man who had received the five talents brought the other five. "Master," he said, "you entrusted me with five talents.

See, I have gained five more."

His master replied, "Well done, good and faithful servant! You have been faithful with a few things; I will put you in charge of many things. Come and share your master's happiness!"
— Matthew 25:19-21

SECTION IV
Promoter's Paradise

CHAPTER THIRTY

"Man, Have I Got a Deal for You!"

As a boy, reared on the farm, I had many enlightening experiences. I have been to hog killings, cattle dippings, goat ropings, pig markings, turkey shoots, rat killings, mad-dog chases, horse breakings,

log rollings, all-day singings, and dinners-on-the-ground; however, none of these prepared me for the true stories that I'll be sharing with you.

Once again, "If it sounds too good to be true, it probably is." Make an indelible mental note of this saying in your brain, because you will need to remember it many times in life. Just about everyone is a sucker when offered "something for nothing." Our politicians learned this a long time ago and know what to say to get elected.

Barnham and Bailey said, "There's a sucker born every minute." And I've got more news for you: there is an unscrupulous promoter born every ten seconds. That makes six promoters for every sucker.

Dream peddlers, peddling elusive big deals, constantly rise to the surface. From gold mines to oil wells, they are always there with a "no-way-to-lose" hot deal just for you.

The Milkens, Boskys, and a few big Wall Street firms grab the headlines, but it's the boiler room "scammers" that take the lifetime savings out of the pockets of unsuspecting, gullible investors.

It is absolutely amazing how they can come up with forty-seven dozen different ways to skin a cat. In my fifty years in retail, real estate, and other various businesses, I have come across some first-class, award-winning "doozies."

Hundreds of deal makers have sniffed me out over these fifty years. Let me tell you about just a few of the "fantastic" deals they have pitched me. File these stories away in your mind, because you will face similar "big deals" in your life. Maybe a little bell will go off and you'll remember the line, "If it sounds too good to be true, it probably is."

All the names in these true stories have been changed to protect the "guilty."

The Great Money Chase #1

All businesses need capital from time to time, and there are usually many fine banks and institutions willing to lend money to them. In the early '70s, there was an oil embargo which greatly affected many businesses, placing them in desperate need of capital. While we were suffering, the Mid-East oil-producing nations were rolling in petro-dollars. In fact, it was "running out their ears."

Thousands of American businesses were caught in a credit crunch and could not afford the scandalous interest rates being charged. I know, because our real estate company was caught in an expansion phase, and at one point, we were paying 21 percent interest on borrowed capital.

The stage was set for the unscrupulous promoters to move in and cash in. All they needed was the golden key to unlatch the doors to the American businessman's vault. Sure enough, they found it.

The old song "I've Got the Money If You've Got the Time" was brought out of the juke-box cellars and played in thousands of offices all over America.

Turn the Lights Down Low

Here is how the record played: Promoters claimed to have discovered a new source of funds through their contacts in the oil-rich Arab countries. While American banks were charging ridiculously high rates, funds through these Mid-East sources were said to be available at only 5 to 6 percent interest. To make it even more attractive, it was said you could pay interest only for the first ten years. What a deal! It seemed just too good to be true. Does that ring a bell? These Arabs were

said to be dying to loan out all their billions. You would
see them at airports everywhere, and you just knew
they were closing deals and loaning out billions
everyday.

Page 2
So the printing presses went into high gear.
Beautiful, well-done, professional packages were mailed
out to thousands of businesses—some from well-known
and respected brokers who somehow were caught up in
"the great money chase." Most, however, were from
boiler room operations with a bank of phones or just a
slick operator with a briefcase and a little traveling
money.

Old Friends Never Die, They Just Keep Calling

Well, it wasn't long until I got a call from an old friend we'll call "Herby." He had a pretty good reputation as a deal maker. He had been reasonably successful in the insurance and investment brokerage business and was fairly well-known in our area. He invited me to meet an Arab sheik who was coming to the United States. Herby told me the sheik would fly in to meet me and would offer all the money we needed at, of course, a fantastic interest rate. He had billions and must get them loaned out. In fact, his family was the wealthiest family in the world. Since we were a fast-growing discount store chain and expanding rapidly this sounded fantastic.

A Real Sheik

The date was set, and I drove over to a local hotel to meet the Arab sheik. I had already heard about these big deals and, frankly, was quite skeptical, but there was nothing to lose and everything to gain. I entered the room and, sure enough, there he was in all his Arab attire waiting with my old friend, Herby. We were introduced and were soon overwhelmed by the tales of billions of dollars this Arab family controlled. Herby was so impressed he could hardly contain himself. The sheik did seem like a solid, upright Arab gentleman—very religious, too. In fact, we had to stop our discussion while our friendly Arab banker faced Mecca and prayed.

The meeting was finally concluded, and he was off to New York for other meetings. I requested a multi-million dollar loan package. After all, if we didn't need that much money, I could put what was left into a bank C.D. and make double the interest we would be paying.

In the Bag

Old Herby assured me that we would get the loan and that he would get back to me later with the details.

This all sounded "too good to be true," but I had nothing to lose, and I was determined to find out what was behind all this Mid-East oil money and these low-interest loans.

Why would people spend thousands of dollars to fly all over the world, make numerous overseas telephone calls, and prepare such fancy literature if it were not real?

Well, hold on to this one for now, while I tell you about the next great "money chase."

The Great Money Chase #2

Another old friend of mine, I'll call him "Wilbur," was also caught up in "The Great Money Chase." He called me and said he and a friend, who was an ex-professional football player, had lined up a large source of Mid-East money through a broker in New York.

I said to myself, "Let's find out what this game is all about. Let's borrow a few million at 5 percent interest from him, too."

A Bite of the Apple

I called our company pilot and told him to gas up the Jet Commander, as we were heading to New York City. We took off early in the morning with Wilbur and landed in New York City to pick up two more men who somehow fit into the picture (they could have passed for members of the Mafia). We flew on to Buffalo, where we were chauffeured out to a rural area and escorted into a spacious home with exquisite offices. We were served a delicious meal and quickly led into a discussion about our needs and their desire to make loans. The only argument seemed to be whether we would pay 5 or 6 percent interest. We finally gave in to 6 percent and were assured that we had a deal. During our conversation, our host was continually talking on the phone—supposedly with people in Geneva and other big-money centers. We were also constantly interrupted by his secretary with calls about big deals from everywhere imaginable. We could hear them in the adjoining room with much of the conversation in a foreign language. The place was a beehive of activity, London calling . . . Geneva . . . Rome . . . .

The Real Thing

Man, we were finally where the action was. This had
to be real. This operation cost big bucks, and they could
not possibly be paying the tab unless they were making
loans.

Yet, there was always that nagging feeling that
something just did not add up. Why the bargain-
basement interest rate?

Well, we left assured that it was as good as done and
headed home. Very soon, telexes began to come in . . .
and things really looked good.

The Mystery of the Great Money Chase

After several months of involvement, the puzzle finally came together. The deals we were involved in represented only a small tip of the iceberg. During that same time period, many other similar deals came across my desk and across the desks of thousands of other businessmen all over the nation.

All told, millions of man hours were lost and vast sums of money were spent. Not only were many businessmen sucked in, but also some sincere brokers got caught up in the great money chase.

In the end, no money was ever loaned to a single person. There never was any money or rich Arabs who wanted to loan mega bucks at ridiculously low interest rates.

The big question was, who paid to keep the front up and who profited?

The Scam

During those times, there was a large number of businesses that were short on cash and needed to borrow money. The exorbitant high interest rates made it impossible for these businesses to borrow funds through normal banking channels. The crooked promoters saw the opportunity. The need was there, and the customer was hungry. It was the perfect setup, and the trap was sprung.

The Inside Scoop

It worked like this: A sharp promoter would open a plush office in a prestigious locale—let's say London, Paris, Geneva, or New York. He would partner up with an Arab or Mid-East personality with the right accent.

All dressed up in their Arab attire and with the proper protocol, they would bring the office alive with activity. They would hire employees of similar background, who may not have been aware of the true intentions of the partners. These employees did much of the legwork and the day-to-day routine activities.

The printing presses began to roll out professional, high-quality packets and brochures. They were mailed to every known broker and contact in the United States. High-sounding financial names were listed on the letterhead. Branch offices were listed in major world financial centers, along with telex numbers and phone numbers. They had it all. The air of respectability and genuineness was stamped all over the operation. The potential customers who might fly over to visit their office would be impressed.

If asked about the low interest rates, their pitch would follow this line: "We represent some oil-rich Arab sheiks who do not use the normal banking channels. They are extremely sensitive about their wealth, so for tax and other obvious reasons, we handle their investments. We are looking to make contacts with American brokers and businessmen who can place or use these large sums. For our special clients, like yourself, our money sources are asking only 5 percent interest."

How Can I Get in on This?

You can imagine the response such an offer generated. Soon, brokers all over the country were bombarding businessmen with the prospect of large sums of money at unheard-of interest rates. Filling station attendants to homemakers joined in the pitch to loan these big funds at low interest rates.

I know of some brokers who believed in these deals so strongly that they spent thousands of their own dollars

on telephone calls and travel, in addition to many hours chasing down customers to apply for these loans.

The Clincher

After the prospect was all fired up about the certainty of the loan, he was told that there would be a fee of up to 5 percent that would be deducted at the time the loan was finalized. This, of course, was a normal procedure in all loans of this nature. Five hundred thousand dollars for closing costs on a $10 million loan that would save $1 million the first year in interest alone was no problem. This was a psychological trick to make it sound as if the loan was approved and ready to be funded.

The borrower was then told that there was only one thing standing in the way of getting the loan closed—a one-time finder's fee of $25,000. This fee would cover expenses for all the travel required, for telexes, telephone calls, printing, overhead, and the presentation of the borrower's loan package. (The fee could be as high as $50,000, depending on the size of the fish on the line.)

The borrower reviews all the correspondence. He is convinced that all is on the up and up. What is $25,000 on a $10 million deal? He has been waiting now for three to five months. He is relying on the loan, and it's urgent that it be funded at once. He wires the $25,000 as directed, sits back, and waits for the loan funds to come to his bank. Suddenly, the phone stops ringing, except for the American promoter who, in some cases, wasn't in on the scam and is waiting for his finder's fee.

The Smoking Gun

Finally they call London, and the secretary tells them the boss is out to close a big loan and will be back in a few days. After a month or so of continuous run-around, suddenly the Arab lender has closed his London office and cannot be found. The scam has succeeded, and he moves on to a new location under a new name to begin all over again.

How much was the take? Out of the thousands of possible contacts who responded, it would not be unreasonable to assume that several hundred were convinced and paid the $25,000 fee to close the deal. Just four hundred victims would yield $10 million. The promoter may have spent half a million to cover his overhead, thus making a cool $9.5 million for six months' work. Not too bad for the scammer. But "too good to be true" for the victims.

Other Sources

While the Mid-East, oil-rich countries had been portrayed as the sources for these mega-loans, lesser-known sources have also cropped up. Since the late 1980s, the country of Panama has become a haven for scammers. These con artists not only promise big loans, but have moved up a notch to offer private placements for stock in newly, emerging companies.

Their money-eating machine is fueled by gullible and innocent clients seeking funds for their companies and projects. These scammers may even advertise in respectable newspapers and magazines. The recruited prospect is conned into paying big retainer fees for "legal work," the writing of business plans, loan documents, and other expenses. There are cases where unsuspecting clients have been promoted out of $150,000 and more.

Never respond to any advertisement promising big, easy loans, unless you have qualified, professional counsel. This is doubly true for any so-called foreign brokers and agents, no matter how first-rate they may seem to be. Remember, if it sounds to good to be true, it probably is!

The lesson for your money tree: there's always a price to pay for something worthwhile. There is no such thing as something for nothing—or next to nothing.

The Great Antifreeze Chase

Back in the '70s when the oil embargo was on, you could hardly buy a gallon of antifreeze at any price. Prices skyrocketed, so guess what? Right. The promoters smelled "green" and moved in to supply all the antifreeze needs.

There's Good News Tonight

Guess who called me? Yep. Old "Herby," my friend, who was just about ready to close on our first Arab money deal. Somehow, Herby always seemed to be at the right place at the right time. This time, he had a source for five million gallons of antifreeze at $4.50 per gallon. The going price, if you could find a gallon, was around $8. "Sounds too good to be true." Did we want it? Of course we did. We hardly had a gallon in our nearly one hundred discount stores, so I put him in touch with our automotive buyer.

A Booming Business

The next thing I knew, we began to get telexes from a broker who had sold three million gallons of antifreeze for us that we didn't have. The sale was to some big dealer somewhere, the money was ready to be wired to us, and all we had to do was simply telex him our bank account number and instructions on how to wire the money.

Well, that's quite a sale. The only problem is, we didn't have three million gallons to sell anyone. The price he was willing to pay, according to the broker, was $6.50 per gallon.

So with this impending sale, we had better get busy and get that five million gallons at $4.50 per gallon at

once. We would make $2 per gallon on three million gallons. A tidy $6 million profit. Not bad for one day's work!

So once again, telexes began to fly, coupled with telephone conversations with Herby, the buyer, and the broker. They "confirmed" that the five million gallons were in a freighter sitting in the Port of Houston waiting for permission to unload into our trucks and, of course, we needed to wire money to them in payment.

Running Hot

I was brought up to date on the two deals by our buyer, and I suggested that he had better look very carefully under every rock, as something smelled a little funny about this deal. And it didn't smell like antifreeze—especially since we were supposed to be wiring funds to some offshore bank. I finally told our buyer to break off all conversation on this deal as I was sure there was no antifreeze in the Port of Houston and really no buyer for three million gallons. As soon as we broke off conversation with the broker, we began to get telexes demanding that we fulfill our contract to sell three million gallons to an unidentified buyer. We, of course, responded that we had signed no commitment to sell anyone three million gallons of antifreeze, as we had none to sell, and of course there was no antifreeze in the port of Houston to be bought by anyone at any price.

Tell Me It's a Dream

A few days later we were served with a $30 million lawsuit alleging that we broke a contract to sell three million gallons of antifreeze. Now you don't take any lawsuit lightly, so we had an attorney check out this broker/dealer. Sure enough, he turned out to be a fellow in a one-room office with a telephone, and it was obvious that he was a fake. He had concocted this story about the antifreeze in the Port of Houston. Out of this nonexistent anti-freeze, he had sold three million gallons through us to a nonexistent buyer. Our attorney advised us it was strictly a nuisance lawsuit and that there was no way for the character to win. We eventually settled for $3,000 just to stop the hassles.

Selling It by the Shiploads

Well, it's "Wilbur" on the phone again with another big deal. This time, Wilbur has met a cousin of King Faisal of Saudi Arabia.

The king's cousin had contacts with big companies in Kuwait, Saudi Arabia, and other oil-rich countries. This cousin wanted to arrange for us to export all kinds of commodities, from toothpaste to electrical appliances, to the big Mid-East companies. Of course, we had access to everything he wanted through companies we already did business with. We could supply all they could pay for. Money was no problem for them, as the oil dollars were flowing wide open.

Toothpaste for "Camels"

So my friend, Wilbur, set up an appointment with the Arab cousin of King Faisal. The meeting was to take place in my office. At the appointed time, the Arab arrived, all dressed up in his Arab attire, accompanied by my friend Wilbur. He was well-educated and spoke English well. In fact, he had married an American and was now living in the United States. He had all his credentials and, sure enough, was a cousin of King Faisal. (I later learned that the kings have numerous cousins because of their many wives, so just about everybody is a cousin.)

His presentation was well-organized. He spoke with authority and was very impressive. It was obvious that he was a real businessman and had genuine, royal blood flowing through his veins.

He said his family was not only interested in our commodities, but also in buying real estate in the United States. Well, we assured him that we could supply him all the toothpaste and other commodities he needed. In fact, we would even supply toothpaste for all their camels, if they wanted us to. And we could certainly help him in the real estate field, as we were also real estate developers. His deal "sounded too good to be true," right?

A Night in the Royal Palace

He set a date for us to fly to the Mid-East with him to visit the oil-rich "top dogs" and to meet his cousin, King Faisal. Hopefully, we would even get to spend the night in the royal palace.

Why should we not believe him? He had his credentials. He certainly was a full-blooded Arab. He was a first-class gentleman, and he was obviously well-heeled financially. Should we go? At the very least, it would be a unique experience and we really didn't have much to lose. It might just turn out to be a winner. A night in "the king's palace" would be a great story to tell our grandkids.

I updated my passport and even got the necessary immunizations. He said our trip would take two to three weeks and that he would stay another thirty to sixty days to work out the details for the importing.

The Camels Became Restless

Just before we finalized our reservations, our Arab friend came over for a final meeting. He wanted to review our presentation to make sure everything was in good order. He quickly took charge of the meeting, asking questions and reviewing our presentation. Finally, he began to discuss the actual trip.

We had been under the impression that we would be accompanying him and that he would pay his own way. But get ready for this: He wanted us to purchase his airfare tickets, advance him $10,000, and pay for all his expenditures during his extended stay after our return. This, of course, could ultimately add up to be quite a tidy sum. The bottom line was that he wanted to go home, and he had concocted this whole scheme to accomplish his goal.

This brought to an end our brief experience in the exporting business. Those poor camels never got their toothpaste.

The Greatest "Deal of All Deals"

He who works his land will have abundant food,
but the one who chases fantasies
will have his fill of poverty.
— Proverbs 28:19

You guessed it; it's old "Herby" again. I hadn't heard from him in a while, but now he had run across the "grand-daddy deal of all deals," one that would surpass General Motors and generate billions of dollars.

This time, his deal was presented in letter form. There was no telephone call or visit to my office. You would not believe the opportunity in this fantastic deal, so I'm letting you read the letter, word for word, just as he sent it to me. I have only deleted his real name and a few other names and places.

September 27, 1978

Mr. Alton Howard, President
Howard Bros. Discount Stores
Monroe, LA 71201

Dear Alton,

We are privileged to present reliable information on the "Power Source," a portable power plant that defies all existing laws of physics, Ohms Law, etc. Its characteristics will astound you. Mr. _____, the inventor, is originally from _____, and I know you will be impressed with him.

This fantastic invention is a compact portable unit of approximately 3½ ft. x 3 ft. high. The device is capable of generating 360 amps or 220 volts of electricity and weighs 200 lbs. It will plug into any existing household electrical plug, after outside power has been disconnected, and it will supply more than enough electrical power for an entire home.

The device will supply sufficient electricity to operate a small business or a complete farm. It generates this power and keeps its starting battery recharged. It is maintenance free, air cooled, noiseless, and uses no outside power supply. The device will provide power continuously for approximately 10 years without replacing parts. A 10-year warranty will be issued. The device has capabilities of supplying power to remote areas immediately, and emergency power for hospitals, clinics, etc. It has diversified uses and is pollution free. The device has been built, tested, proven, and is now a reality. The pilot device has operated successfully for more than two years.

We also have built an automobile engine powered by a unit similar to the above, which is controlled by a rheostat. Its size and weight is one-fourth that of a Cadillac 472 engine and its power is comparable. It is capable of cruising at 7,000 r.p.m. and has 412 horsepower; the engine can be adapted to fit into any auto, truck, tractor, boat, forklift, earth-moving equipment, or prop-type aircraft. This engine will be invaluable in solving the energy crisis.

We have already received offers for the exclusive marketing rights in several states for $100,000 each. You should immediately get with your attorney and consult with our lawyer and the inventor. Then you must come see the pilot device which has been in operation for over two years and also inspect the engine which is operative.

We will build the factory on the Gulf Coast for convenience in overseas

shipping. If you will provide the one
million dollars for start-up operation,
which will be repaid to you in full, plus
interest, within 2 years, then we can
safely predict that in 10 years you will
be one of the wealthiest men in America,
if not the world.

These are two of the greatest
inventions of the 20th Century. The
possibilities of amassing great wealth
with them is very real. You are cognizant
of the fact that Fortune knocks at every
man's door once in a lifetime, and I am
confident that you have the expertise and
the acuity to detect the feasibility of
this extraordinary opportunity. The
inventor deserves the eternal gratitude
of a grateful nation because he has
invented a machine that will augment the
power of men and the well-being of
mankind.

We want you on our team to assure
incredible success and to participate in
the financial rewards. The magnitude of
our venture is beyond comprehension.

       With kindest regards, I remain.
       Very sincerely yours,

       "Herby"

       P.S. This situation is tailored
precisely for you and Jack.

Obviously, I never responded to this letter.

I felt sorry for my old friend, Herby, and at the same
time, I had to admire him. One thing was sure, he was
not a quitter. He was a master salesman. He never gave
up, even though the circumstances under which he
wrote this letter were not the best. I have deleted
Herby's return address and identification numbers that
designate his residence as the federal penitentiary.

Old Herby was a pretty nice sort of a fellow, but he
was too quick to believe all those promoters with their

get-rich-quick schemes, and somewhere along the way, he stepped over the line of the law.

I honestly liked Herby and will miss his big deals. They were always exciting, even though they were "too good to be true."

There are a lot of big fish out there that use the Herbys of the world; and they are not in jail. They are the real masterminds behind all these schemes, and they are just waiting to pluck your money tree with some deal that "sounds too good to be true."

They Will Find You

Dateline: St. Francis Hospital, Monroe, Louisiana, February 14, 1990. I was lying in a hospital bed with pneumonia, minding my own business, when a neatly-dressed gentleman walked in. I'll call him "Willie." Willie appeared to be about sixty-five years old, and he had maps showing the location of hidden gold treasure in New Mexico worth $2 billion and uncirculated coins worth $150 million. He needed only $5 million to buy the land. If I would put up the $5 million, I would then own 50 percent of the deal.

At the moment, all he really needed was enough money to buy a motor home to get there. I really believe the gentleman believed what he was saying. Probably, someone had taken his last dollar in exchange for this "bill of goods," and he was hoping to find a pot of gold at the end of the rainbow.

How Do You Escape?

I have had them call me in the middle of the night, hunt me down on business trips, wave me down on the highway, pull me over at red lights, chase me down in pickup trucks, come to my home unannounced, catch me in parking lots, sit down at my table in restaurants (and even put their meals on my check), grab me at airports, show up at church, and generally just make my day.

It was a cold February day and my wife, Jean, was giving me my prescribed physical therapy, when our doorbell rang. Jean went to the door, and a nice, polite gentleman asked to speak to me. She invited him to make himself comfortable while she finished my therapy.

After a few minutes, I entered the room to greet our guest. Now get ready for this one. Sitting there in my den was my hospital visitor, Willie. It had been one year, almost to the day, since his last visit, and he was still trying to raise money to dig up that gold treasure. I could not shake Willie's belief that the gold was really there, and he left believing I had turned down the chance of a lifetime.

The Answer

How can you get away from all these fellows? After fifty years of listening, dodging, and getting stung by a few, I think I have finally come up with the answer.

Have your name listed in the obituary column of your newspaper. Put in your picture, and give all the pertinent details of your death, then hope that all the big-deal promoters read it. Surely they would not disturb the dead!

CHAPTER THIRTY-ONE

"Golden Opportunities," "No-Way-to-Lose" Deals

*It makes a big difference whether the shepherd is
interested in the flock or the fleece.*

In this chapter, I have listed an additional twenty-three "golden opportunities" that have knocked on my door over the years. My purpose in sharing these true propositions is to let you see the many varied ways you can get "pitched."

By the way, some of these plans might have actually worked—if I had wanted to take the risk, if I had had enough time, and if I owned Fort Knox!

The Who-Eee Stick

One day a man walked into my office with an unusual invention. It was a round stick about twelve inches long. One side was flat with small notches cut across it, and a windmill-like propellor was attached to one end. He was also carrying another stick about six inches long.

He informed me that this was a "who-eee stick." He began to rub the small stick up and down the flat side of the other stick and said, "Who-eee, who-eee, who-eee."

After a few who-ees the propellor began to twirl. Well, I wanted to give this who-eee thing a try and, sure enough, after a few who-ees it started to twirl for me, too.

Well, this got the attention of my secretary, and soon we were all having a "who-eee" good time. I'm glad my banker didn't walk in about this time. However, if my friend Sam Walton can do a Hawaiian dance dressed in a hula skirt on Wall Street, I guess a little who-eee party in Monroe, Louisiana, would not have been too wild for me!

Let's All Do the Who-Eee
I might have really missed a whing-dinger of an opportunity here. I should have lined up all our office

employees, passed out who-eee sticks, called in our advertising department, and filmed a television spot on the new "who-eee stick" craze. "A whole lot of who-eee going on!" Can't you just see every office in America doing the who-eee at every coffee break? No telling what the kids at school would have done with this who-eee stick.

Now don't laugh. One fellow took a plastic tube a few years back and made millions. You recall, of course, the Hula-Hoop craze that even made chiropractors rich. Then came along the "clackers" that made a few million until they started chipping and putting out eyes. And don't forget the pet rock craze and the many others that came along the way. Compared to all these, I would rate the who-eee stick pretty high. The inventors of all these others laughed, too—all the way to the bank.

But I just couldn't convince myself to invest in the who-eee stick. Really, its name sounded too much like Papa when he used to call the hogs back on our little farm in Rocky Branch. All I could see was a bunch of hogs charging through the woods to get to the feed trough.

A COW MANURE PACKAGING PLANT

A $25 million deal that smelled like too much bull for me. I just didn't have the taste for that one.

THE OIL DRILLING BUSINESS

Too many dry holes—too few oil spills.

POTTING-SOIL FACTORY

Buying a swamp in Louisiana and selling the dirt as potting soil. Sounded too much like a "dirty" deal to me.

GOLD RUSH

Mining gold in Nevada. Billions in the mountains just waiting to be dug out. My shovel wasn't big enough for this one.

SQUEEZING OIL OUT OF SHALE DEPOSITS

The problem was, they could squeeze all the gold out of your bank deposits before they could squeeze any oil out of the rock deposits.

THE SEARCH FOR PANCHO VILLA'S TREASURE

I really think Pancho spent it all before we arrived.

THE SEARCH FOR NOAH'S ARK

I do believe it is there, but it's gonna take another flood to float it out.

URANIUM MINE IN COLORADO

This one was too "hot" to handle!

PERPETUAL-MOTION MACHINE

We already had some of those in our stores. "Look at those mouths!"

A SEARCH FOR
THE TITANIC

I got to go down below deck on the search ship, but there was a "loose screw" on the top deck.

GRAVEL MINING

This one was the "pits," and the guys running it had "rocks" in their heads.

TIMES SQUARE BUILDING FOR SALE

I could have had my choice of vending space, but I just didn't have enough $peanuts$ for this one.

WORLD FOOTBALL LEAGUE

Name of the team: "The Texans." Everything is "big" in Texas, and this one lived up to it—"a big, big flop."

ANTIQUES FROM THE MID-EAST

We probably would have stored them in Kuwait for "safe keeping" before the Persian-Gulf war.

CRAWFISH FARM

Afraid I might get pinched on this one.

COAL MINE IN TENNESSEE

You needed a whole lot of "coal cash" for this endeavor.

PEA-SHELLING FACTORY

"I'll pass on the peas, please."

CORN-MILLING PLANT

Sounded like a lot of "chops" for the "birds" peddling this deal.

25,000-ACRE COLORADO WHEAT FARM

Plenty of bread on the table, but none in your pocket.

SILK SUITS FROM HONG KONG

All dressed up and nowhere to go! The promoter's and associates' names seemed prophetic—"Dong Gong Wong Tune."

VITAMIN PYRAMID

To keep up with this one you had better take plenty of them.

THINKERS AND SITTERS

Of all the deals that I have been pitched along the way, I believe this one is the funniest of all, and I must share it with you.

A really nice lady called one day and said she had an invention that she felt could do well. She had been told by some of my friends at Rocky Branch that I might have an interest in manufacturing and developing her invention. It was something that went around the "ordinary bathroom toilet." She said, and I quote, *"This is something I've been sitting on for a long time."*

Well, I needed a little time to sit on this one, too.

THE ENTREPRENEUR

Lest I leave the impression that all entrepreneurs are wild promoters seeking to waylay the public, I hasten to add that this is not my intention, nor is it true.

The spirit of the entrepreneur has been and still is a driving force in the success of the American free-enterprise system. Most successful, major American companies owe their beginning to the American entrepreneur. Multiplied thousands of small firms, the backbone of American business, were founded and are operated by such men and women, all a result of their creative spirit.

New ideas and new ways to do the "impossible" flow from the hands and minds of those who are not content with the status quo. A vast resource of talent and ideas would never be tapped should this spirit be stifled and crushed. This spirit should be encouraged and applauded by citizens and government alike.

I tip my hat to these entrepreneurs, these men and women of undominable spirit, who keep inventing new products and keep finding new ways to "build a better mouse trap."

Sure-fire test to prove you have a winner:
When seven out of ten say,
"Well, I'll be doggone, why didn't I think of that!"

The Original Discounters

SUMMARY

A Final Look

In this final look, I wish to reflect on some thoughts that will make a vast difference to you in building your money tree.

First of all, never forget that true success is not measured in pure dollars and cents. There are "rich" failures everywhere—men and women who sacrificed loving families and lasting relationships to gain the fantasy called the "American Dream." The richness of life cannot be captured in one drab shade of green but only by a vast array of colors that blend and fill the whole portrait of your life.

Second of all, use your money in productive and constructive ways. If you allow yourself to waste your resources foolishly, the peace and freedom you destroy will be your own; and the lives you could have blessed will never experience your generosity.

Last of all, never forget that God made life a wonderful, exciting, and challenging journey. Yes, there are some storms along the way, but this journey is also filled with extraordinary rainbows. I trust that from the pages of this book you have gained encouragement, confidence, and skills that will enable you to sail through the storms and experience the rainbows.

To all on this journey, I dedicate the following about memories. May your ascent to the mountain peak be a debt-free, happy, exciting, successful climb, and may your money tree yield bountiful fruit in every season.

Footprints in the Mind

Memories—a gift of God: footprints in the mind, ties to our past. They remind us of our roots, our struggles, our victories, and our tears. These footprints are imprinted in our minds when, in a split second, beauty and eternity are frozen into our consciousness. Like a frozen stream, they bubble up around the rocks, running deep under the surface of our mind.

Life is like a climb up a lofty mountain—a mountain both beautiful and treacherous. This mountain has two peaks.

Our climb up that first peak began with Mom and Dad holding our hands. Those were carefree, innocent, happy days, filled with home, church, family, supper time, birthdays, Santa Claus, and laughter. It was a time when we sat beside them in church and heard them sing their songs. We also sat by the fireside with Grandma and Grandpa, spellbound as we listened to stories they had heard from their parents—stories that span generations. Something great was happening and we were unaware.

As we continued up that first peak, we came to realize that there was something beyond our small circle of home. We looked around and saw other mountains to climb. In time, the challenge became so strong that we felt like the little bird in his comfortable nest, who, after looking over the edge, perches himself, stretches his neck, flaps his untested wings, and finally takes a leap into uncertainty. We packed up our few belongings and said good-bye to Mom and Dad. With a song on our lips, we were confident that we could conquer the world. We were unaware that as Mom and Dad stood beside us, their hearts were thumping in their breasts. They hid their tears from us because they knew the time had come for their little boy or girl to say good-bye. For months they had known that the days of our childhood were almost over, while we naively feasted in God's sunshine.

The second peak we climb is more difficult and challenging. The road signs are confusing. We now must pull from that deep well of foundational principles, rooted there by Mom and Dad. Like shafts of light in early morning sunrise, those "Footprints in the Mind" burst forth all along the way. When danger lurks ahead of us, we can look back down the slope to the first peak and see those golden shafts of memory; and they give us enough joy and determination to keep climbing.

In time, the climb gets a little harder. We can't see as clearly, hear as well, or walk as fast. There is a clock built into us, and it is running down. We evaluate our climb more carefully: Is my compass set correctly? Have I traveled the right trails? Eternity is just beyond, and we can't rewind the clock! The sun hides behind the peak, and it is dark. The dancing, sparkling lights of those old memories now take a stronger hold and pull us back, back down the slope to childhood days, to the way it once was. We walk down the old trail and recall the fires of home, church, and family. We wish we could live them all over again, but we can't. Those golden shafts, shadows of memory, flood the soul. They are all there, in a moment of time, frozen in consciousness. These footprints are not meant to take us back for long; they are the sparks that fire us on up to the final peak.

Gradually, the markings of the path become unclear, and then the path seems almost to end. Suddenly, in a glorious burst of shooting rays, the top of the peak is aglow with fire! The sun no longer is hidden from our view! We are on the summit!

Our spirit soars! For the first time, the two mountain peaks of present and past merge together. We look back down the slope and see the path more clearly. The path that seemed to be lit only by flickering candles is now aglow with dazzling lights. The trail had been going upward all the time, and we had been lovingly guided by unseen hands.

A new day has dawned, and we are in eternity with God! Faith has brought victory! Home at last! Thank God for memories! Footprints in the mind!

© Alton H. Howard

Appendix

Instructions for
Net Worth Statement

In order to grow a healthy money tree, you must
know where you stand financially. Determine your net
worth by completing the following *Net Worth Statement*.
If your liabilities exceed your assets, you are in trouble.
Your goal must be to increase your income, control your
expenses, and reduce your debts in order to   create   a
positive net worth. Remember to count only the actual,
depreciated sell value of all you own. What would your
car bring if you had to sell it today?

At the bottom of this page is a prayer. By
acknowledging that all you have belongs to God, you
will gain a new, healthier perspective toward money
and wealth.

*Dear God, father and creator of us all, sustainer and
giver of all things: I want to acknowledge that all I
have is yours. Help me to be a good manager of all that
you have entrusted into my care.*

Signed _____

_____

Net Worth Statement

Your assets

Savings accounts _____

Checking accounts _____

Certificates of Deposit _____

U.S. Savings Bonds _____

Life insurance (cash value) _____

Annuities (surrender value) _____

Pension (vested interest) _____

Securities (market value) _____

Real estate (market value) _____

Business interests _____
   (market value—net of debt)

Personal property _____
   (jewelry, auto, etc.)

Other _____

Total assets: _____

Your liabilities

Home mortgage (prin. balance) _____

Car loans (principle balance) _____

Installment loans (prin. balance) _____

Charge account balances _____

Other _____

Total liabilities: _____

+Total assets _____

-Total liabilities _____

= Net Worth _____

Instructions for
Budget Worksheets

The following worksheets are to be used to prepare a realistic budget and help you stick to it. Begin with the **Budget Worksheet.** Figure what you have available to spend each month. If you are paid every two weeks, multiply your biweekly paycheck by 26 and divide by 12 to get your monthly take-home pay. If you are paid on the 1st and 15th, simply multiply your paycheck by two. If you receive any annual bonuses, commissions, or other once-a-year income, it is best not to include these amounts in your calculations. You will not have these funds available for monthly use. Use these funds to add to your savings or to pay for extraordinary, unexpected expenses. (Note: If you have a small business that you operate out of your home or have rental property, include the *net* cash inflow on the *Business Income* line. If your business has a negative cash flow, then include this outgo on the *Business Outgo* line as an expense.) Think of every dollar you spend and put it somewhere in the *Monthly Outgo* section. The absolutely essential monthly payments (house note or rent, utilities, transportation, insurance, contributions, etc.) should be entered first. If your total monthly outgo is less than your total monthly income, then put the difference on the *Savings* line so the total will equal your monthly income. (Always be sure you actually save this money.) If your total monthly outgo exceeds your monthly income, you must adjust your planned spending to make them equal.

If you don't know where you've been, you can't know where you're going. It is imperative that you know where every penny goes. Use the **Weekly Spending Record** to keep a tight rein on your spending. Keep a small spiral notebook in your purse or carry a piece of paper and pen in your pocket. Write down every dollar as you spend it and what you spend it on. (By the way, you must balance your checking account daily and reconcile it each month to know where you stand and make sure your balance is correct. This is a must!) At the end of each week, write down the total you spent for each category on your *Weekly Spending Record*. Watch your *Weekly Spending Record* closely to see that your monthly totals do not exceed the monthly outgo total from your *Budget Worksheet*. If you see that your spending may exceed your budget plan, adjust your spending immediately. As you begin keeping the actual figures, you will be able to refine your plan and be better able to budget future months.

At the end of every month, prepare the **Budget to Actual Comparison** to compare your actual spending to your planned spending. Enter what you planned to spend in each category in the column marked *Budget*. You can get these numbers from the *Monthly Outgo* section of our completed *Budget Worksheet*. Enter the *Total* column from your *Weekly Spending Record* in the *Actual* column on your *Budget to Actual Comparison*. If you go over in any category, you must subtract this amount from the next month's plan. If you underspend, you should save the money for future contingencies. If your spending gets out of line or your income decreases, cut back immediately. Delay will only make the problem worse. Keep your *Weekly Spending Record* and *Budget to Actual Comparison* sheets in a safe place. Next year, they will be very helpful in planning the new year and charting your progress in achieving your goal of freedom from financial worry.

Budget Worksheet
Part 1
Monthly Income

● Your take-home pay   _____

● Spouse's take-home pay   _____

● Bonuses   _____

● Commissions   _____

● Tips   _____

● Dividends   _____

● Interest   _____

● Royalties   _____

● Business Income   _____

● Social Security   _____

● Pension Benefits   _____

● Profit-Sharing   _____

● Annuities   _____

● Other   _____

Total monthly income   [_____]

Budget Worksheet
Part 2
Monthly Outgo

- Business outgo _____
- Clothing & laundry _____
- Club dues _____
- Contributions _____
- Entertainment & recreation _____
- Food & drink (at home & out) _____
- Gifts _____
- Hair care _____
- Household maintenance _____
- Household supplies _____
- Installment purchase payments _____
- Insurance, Household _____
- Insurance, Life _____
- Insurance, Medical _____
- Medical care (not covered by ins.) _____
- Miscellaneous _____
- Newspapers, magazines, books _____
- Property taxes _____
- Rent or mortgage payments _____
- Savings _____
- Telephone _____
- Toiletries _____
- Transportation* _____
- Utilities _____

Total monthly outgo [   ]

*Transportation includes car payments, gasoline, oil, maintenance, repairs, auto insurance, bus, subway, etc.

Weekly Spending Record
Month of _____

	Week 1
Business outgo	
Clothing & laundry	
Club dues	
Contributions	
Entertainment & recreation	
Food & drink (at home & out)	
Gifts	
Hair care	
Household maintenance	
Household supplies	
Installment purchase payments	
Insurance, Household	
Insurance, Life	
Insurance, Medical	
Medical care (not covered by ins.)	
Miscellaneous	
Newspapers, magazines, books	
Property taxes	
Rent or mortgage payments	
Savings	
Telephone	
Toiletries	
Transportation*	
Utilities	
Totals	

*Transportation includes car payments, gasoline, oil, maintenance, repairs, auto insurance, bus, subway, etc.

Week 2	Week 3	Week 4	Total

Budget to Actual Comparison
Month of _____

	Budget	Actual	Difference
Business outgo			
Clothing & laundry			
Club dues			
Contributions			
Entertainment & rec.			
Food & drink			
Gifts			
Hair care			
Household maint.			
Household supplies			
Installment payments			
Insurance, Household			
Insurance, Life			
Insurance, Medical			
Medical care			
Miscellaneous			
News, mags., books			
Property taxes			
Rent or mortgage			
Savings			
Telephone			
Toiletries			
Transportation*			
Utilities			
Totals			

*Transportation includes car payments, gasoline, oil, maintenance, repairs, auto insurance, bus, subway, etc.